# *Ways*
# *Teacher's Book*

## Alexander Franklin

*For use with*

# *Ways*

## An Anthology of Verse for Junior Schools

*Compiled by*
Pamela and
Alexander Franklin

*Oliver & Boyd*

Oliver and Boyd
Croythorn House
23 Ravelston Terrace
Edinburgh EH4 3TJ
*A Division of Longman Group Ltd.*

ISBN 0 05 002340 3

First published 1973
© 1973 Alexander Franklin.

Set in 10/12pt Bembo (270)
Printed in Great Britain by
Martin's of Berwick

# Contents

1 The Anthology  1

2 The Teacher and the Class  4

3 Methods:  9
   *(i)*    *Choral Speaking*  9
   *(ii)*   *Movement and Mime*  13
   *(iii)*  *Drama and Dramatisation*  15
   *(iv)*  *Art and Craft*  17
   *(v)*   *Composition*  19
   *(vi)*  *Original Verse*  21
   *(vii)* *Reading*  24

4 Teaching the Verse in Book I  26

5 Teaching the Verse in Book II  41

  Index of Titles  65

  Index of First Lines  72

  Index of Authors  79

# Acknowledgments

The authors and publisher wish to acknowledge the use of copyright material as follows: The extract from 'The Dancing Cabman', from *Speaking Together* by Cobby and Laurie is by permission of Sir Isaac Pitman & Sons Ltd.; and the extract from 'Skipping Song' by John Walsh is by permission of Mrs. M. Walsh. The poem 'Growing' by Joseph Korner on p. 23 is reprinted by permission both of the poet and of his mother, Mrs. Shirley Korner.

# 1 The Anthology

This is a new kind of junior school anthology. It is called WAYS because it provides routes to the appreciation of poetry with verse which lends itself to particular *ways* of teaching. The majority of these are active and involve the children in practical pursuits. Book I is intended for children of about 7 to 9; Book II, for children of about 9 to 11. The demand for the anthology grew out of the success of the present writer's *Choral Verse* (Oliver & Boyd, 1962) which, although intended for secondary schools, has been used extensively in junior education. But in WAYS the scope is wider and, as will be seen, choral speaking is only one of a variety of approaches.

## The Purpose of Teaching Verse

An appreciation of poetry is seldom achieved before adolescence, for it is in part intellectual and it requires some acquaintance with the vast world of poetic experience and the poets' perceptive views of life. Enjoyable contact with verse in earlier years is the ideal preparation.

The teaching of verse can also encourage delight in language, extend vocabulary, and perhaps even show that prose is not always the best way of saying something, let alone the only way. Achievements in these areas are valuable, especially as they help in warding off some of the common prejudices against poetry, but they are ancillary. It is the long-term appreciation of poetry which must be the principal aim of teaching verse in the junior school, and that is why WAYS has been made.

## Contents

The verse has been selected on the strength of its quality, its variety, its suitability for young children, and its value as teaching material. Inevitably, choice has rested heavily upon personal preference. Even though we try to make assessments according to commonly accepted standards, language—and especially patterned language—speaks to each of us differently, and in the end individual taste must count for a good deal. It is particularly difficult for anthologists to use an age yardstick, for age is only one factor in mental achievement, and perhaps the least important. The two books of WAYS are broad collections therefore: some of the pieces in Book I appeal to infants; some in Book II are not inappropriate in secondary schools; the two books themselves do not touch one another so much as overlap. It is teachers, with their personal knowledge of particular children, who must always have the final say. Perhaps only on the question of suitability may the anthologist presume to offer advice, by pointing out that some verse may be acceptable even when the children do not fully understand it. The young child's world is full of things he does not wholly understand—a state of affairs which he accepts as part of life, and which does not spoil his pleasure.

## Special Features of the Selection
Subject has influenced selection hardly at all. The verse has been chosen, regardless of topic, because it is considered to have relevance for junior school children by lying within their experience—actual or imaginative. To find examples of the latter is comparatively easy, but pieces that present-day children can relate to themselves are much harder to come by. It is not simply that their experience is limited, but that there is a regrettable dearth of children's verse stemming from life in the second half of the 20th century. Indeed, many children can be forgiven for thinking that the poet's world is chiefly an agricultural one in which cows are milked by hand and farmers trot to market on grey mares.

WAYS, whilst affording glimpses of the past, romance or magic in, for example, *Here we Come A-Piping* (Book I, p. 2), *Cowboy Spring* (Book I, p. 23), *The Three Singing Birds* (Book I, p. 65) and *The Fugitive* (Book II, p. 83), also contains such pieces as *The Dustman* (Book I, p. 8), *After a Bath* (Book I, p. 57), *Peter to Tea* (Book II, p. 74), *The Helicopter* (Book II, p. 116), and others which have particular significance for present-day children.

As the names of writers do not mean much to junior school children, there has been no attempt to include particular authors merely because they are well-known. Conversely, if, in the search for good and suitable material, certain writers seem to have provided more than their fair share, there has been no question of reducing their quota.

WAYS differs most from other anthologies in that as much consideration has been given to the teaching of the verse as to its intrinsic merits. No piece has been included without at least one way of teaching it being known to the anthologists.

## Ways of Teaching the Verse
Teaching verse is an individual matter. It is affected by factors such as the teacher's knowledge of the class, the facilities of the school, personal experience, and personal preference. Generalisations about the teaching of verse, even when

made in the cause of being helpful, can therefore be misleading. It has to be recognised, though, that junior school teachers are required to handle so many parts of the school curriculum that they are frequently without adequate preparation time, and that, inevitably, there are areas of it where their expertise is slighter than they could wish. In Chapter 2 the principles of employing active methods in teaching verse are discussed, and every piece in the two parts of WAYS is the subject of a note setting out at least one way of teaching it.

None of the notes *specifies* a treatment; they merely recommend approaches which may be found to serve in the absence of something better. It is hoped, though, that teachers will want to use the verse *actively* because not only does this increase the chances of its being enjoyed by the children but it also allows them to be introduced to worthwhile material which would otherwise make no impression upon them. A case in point is *Old Dan'l* by L. A. G. Strong, which is unlikely to appeal to a child of nine or ten if he merely reads it or listens to it. But if it is used with an appropriate visual exercise (such as that suggested in Ch. 5, p. 52), he may then see that its eight short lines are a kind of word snapshot, which in itself is a step towards appreciating word economy as an attribute of poetry.

The various teaching approaches to which the verse seems to lend itself are summarised on p. 7 of Chapter 2. They will be seen to comprise a variety of choral treatments, mime, movement and dramatisation, work in visual media, and oral, prose and verse composition. Also in each book there is a selection of verse which can be taught by nothing more elaborate than straightforward reading. The reason for this is explained on p. 24. What may be worth stating here is that the anthologists have no quarrel with such an orthodox approach (obviously they would not have included the sections 'Listen!' and 'Listen Again!' if they had), but they do maintain (1) that in the primary school the majority of verse is best taught through involving the children actively, (2) that a piece taught by an inactive method needs to be selected with particular care, and (3) as a note headed 'Discussion' on p. 25 suggests, any follow-up to a reading should not be based upon critical analysis.

## Photographs and Drawings

The drawings in the pupils' books relate closely to the verse beside which they are found. The photographs, however, are not intended as illustrations; their purpose is to provoke comment and stimulate creative work. Some have an obvious affinity with particular verse, which they may reinforce or supplement, but in instances where the link between the photographs and the printed word may not be apparent to the children, it is hoped that they will find the pictures make statements in their own right.

# 2 The Teacher and the Class

The following observations relate specifically to the kind of verse contained in WAYS; they are far from being an exhaustive statement on the teaching of verse in general.

## 'Doing' Verse

It is very usual for children to 'do' verse; they work on a piece, and then, when circumstances suggest it, the teacher moves them on to another. They go from verse to verse in the way that visitors to a town 'do' its churches. There is nothing wrong with this; it can provide general impressions of verse, just as the tourist can get general impressions of church architecture. But if the junior school teacher believes that when a child goes on to secondary education he should do so *knowing* a considerable quantity of verse, there is the implication that teaching verse is more than simply 'doing' it. Somewhere along the line, actual learning has to take place.

## Learning Verse

The notes in Chapters 4 and 5 describe a variety of approaches to the verse in both books of this anthology. The methods are intended as a means of introduction, but it is hoped that either the verse itself *or the methods of teaching it* will appeal sufficiently to the children for them to want to continue acquaintanceship with it. Inevitably this means that they will want to use the same verse over and over again—to use a repertory of verse which they come to know well.

## Using a Repertory of Known Verse

It follows, of course, that the teacher must guard against the repertory becoming static. Particularly with the youngest children must he see that they do not develop conservative attitudes. In any event, though, as the children's understanding increases, so may the simplest choices be discreetly dropped and their places taken by more advanced works. But a repertory, a fund of verse in constant use, there should always be.

It is at this stage that books of verse in the classroom become especially necessary. As the notes on particular methods show, there are occasions when a book is an encumbrance, and certainly where children are poor readers, a printed verse, far from being a potential delight, is merely a potential chore. But when verse has been enjoyed through work upon it, it is a simple matter for the child to turn to it in the book and to taste its delights again—and again. Using the repertory does not, of course, rule out the revival of the original introductory method, provided it is suited to repetition. Speaking verse chorally and other ways involving the class corporately are the best for this.

## Learning by Heart

There can be nothing against the idea of committing worthwhile verse to memory; but learning by heart is a method, not an end, and unless one can see some virtue in adopting a tedious process when an enjoyable one can produce the same or better results, there is nothing to be said for it.

## Learning by Involvement

As was pointed out in Chapter 1, most of the verse in WAYS has been chosen because it can be taught through involving the children practically. There is no better principle on which to base junior school teaching, and its application to verse, though not yet widely practised, is consistent with present-day teaching in other parts of the curriculum. The extent to which the children can be involved depends a good deal upon their experience. A class accustomed to formal patterns of education will invariably founder if suddenly given the freedom to work unaided, and even when they are not unfamiliar with the freer approaches, they will usually need some guidance. The aim, though, should always be to have the children working things out as much as possible for themselves.

## Introductions and Explanations

When a new work is to be used, how much should the teacher do by way of introduction? The best way in is normally a reading even when the teaching method is to be choral speaking, a written or a visual exercise, or some other activity. By and large, the less introduction there is the better; the more the children discover of the verse for themselves, the greater the likelihood of its remaining with them. This does not preclude the children's asking questions, of course, but information acquired for a purpose is valued more than that which is given unsolicited. In any case, if by introduction, we have in mind not simply directions as to how the verse may be tackled but explanations of it, it must be pointed out that some verse defies explanation. Could we explain *Here we Come A-Piping* (Book I, p. 2)? If an explanation were offered, would not the verse be destroyed? This charming piece is an extreme example, but many another, rational and logical to an adult mind, makes no such impression on a child. At an age when fact and fantasy merge, children do not look for explanations of everything, nor do they need them. If they have merely the gist of a verse, they can accept it and enjoy it. Usually, only when they cannot grasp the writer's fundamental concept (as perhaps may be the case with a piece like May Swenson's *Water Picture* (Book II, p. 58) is explanation of this kind needed. True, some words may need explaining but if an entire work or a large proportion of it requires explanation, it is probable that the piece is too difficult and it should be abandoned in favour of something else.

It must be said, though, that teachers should not be too ready to work always within the apparent capacity of the children. Unless they are constantly introduced to material which is a little above their current level of attainment and comprehension, children will not advance educationally.

## Integration and Isolation

Many of the ways of teaching verse recommended in Chapters 3, 4 and 5 involve practical skills and include the use of equipment. Teaching of this kind cannot always be fitted conveniently into the period slot of the traditional time-table, and it is suggested that where time is given for verse, as it were, 'officially', it should be used for the less elaborate approaches, and work requiring materials should be integrated with English, art, handwork, as the case may be. (Subject labels do not mean much except administratively; knowledge and experience do not easily break down into subject components.) In the ideal, perhaps, verse should not have its own spot on the time-table at all, but be always brought in with other things, for that is where poetry belongs—in life, not apart from it. It is an attitude which is worth encouraging.

## Singing

Much verse was intended to be sung; the most notable examples in WAYS are, of course, the nursery rhymes. When a verse is known as a song, it is often difficult to detach it from its tune, and there is no reason why one should. Some teachers set verse to tunes composed by themselves or by the children. It is an admirable way of working with verse and music at the same time, but it is not included in the present recommendations because the handling of it requires a specialist's skill.

## Using the Verse in WAYS

It will be seen that each of the two books is divided into sections, and that each section contains verse which can be taught on broadly similar lines. The order of the verse in each section is of no great significance, although generally verse which happens to be on the same topic is grouped together and here and there a progression based on an estimate of difficulty may be detected. It is anticipated that teachers will draw upon the material in whatever order suits their own schemes of work and as they think occasion requires.

## WAYS Summarised

|  | Section Title | Number of Pieces | Approach |
|---|---|---|---|
| **Book I** | **All Together** | 14 | Unison speaking. Simple mime and the use of sound other than speech. |
|  | **One and All** | 14 | Solo speaker(s) and chorus. The use of mime and effects. |
|  | **Parts** | 13 | Simple choral speaking with the class divided into two or more groups. |
|  | **Saying and Doing** | 15 | Choral speaking with activities such as dance, mime and movement. Dramatisation. |
|  | **One Thing and Another** | 19 | Various kinds of art work. Oral and written composition. |
|  | **Listen!** | 20 | Reading aloud. |

| | Section Title | Number of Pieces | Approach |
|---|---|---|---|
| Book II | **Many Voices** | 25 | Simple and more elaborate choral speaking. Mime and dramatisation. |
| | **Hand and Eye** | 21 | A variety of art work (painting, collage, projections, exercises with photographs, etc). Recorded sound. |
| | **Imagine That!** | 27 | Original prose composition (oral and written). |
| | **Models** | 19 | Original verse composition—the limerick, free verse, nonsense verse, etc. |
| | **Listen Again!** | 29 | Reading aloud. |

Many pieces may, of course, be taught in more than one way. They are placed in a particular section according to their most likely use, and reference to other uses is made in the notes.

Detailed comments on the various approaches listed above are contained in Chapter 3.

# 3 Methods

The following comments should be read in conjunction with the notes on individual pieces in Chapters 4 & 5, pages 29 to 40 and pages 44 to 64.

## (i) Choral Speaking

What must be said before anything else is that choral speaking is not considered here for any sort of presentation; above all, it is not intended that it should be used with a public performance in view.

Many educationists are against public performances by junior school children, but, to judge from the number that take place each year, it would seem that a large proportion of practising teachers have no objection to them. One cannot help concluding, however, that the purpose of such performances is not educational at all, but solely to display talents in the name of the school. It is of dubious value. There is probably no great harm in a child's being a member of a choral speaking group on a platform, but it is questionable whether the amount of time spent in rehearsal can be justified; in any case, it is a tedious process which hardly fosters a liking for poetry. As an educational method, which is how choral speaking is seen in the context of this anthology, such questions as cueing and keeping together do not arise; it is the imaginative approach to speaking, based upon the verse itself, which is important. Artistically the efforts of the children may leave much to be desired, but the work is absorbing to those who are doing it, and that is all that matters.

Once the basic principles of speaking in chorus are established, children are usually anxious to suggest the arrangement of the voices, the speed and volume of lines, the deployment of the class, and—provided all these considerations are related to the form and content of the piece to be spoken—it is difficult to think of a more certain way of concentrating the children's attention on the verse. They will get to know the verse without realising they have done so. Naturally, the fullest involvement of the children comes when they are sufficiently familiar with choral speaking for them to handle pieces entirely unaided by the teacher.

## Vocal Arrangements

The following are the principal arrangements for choral speaking suitable for use with junior school children.

1 **Unison Speech.** This is choral speaking in its simplest form. The whole class speaks together. Sometimes a solo voice may act as leader; (see the notes on *The Fifteen Acres*, p. 45).

2 **Soloist(s) and Chorus.** This is particularly valuable with younger children when the verse is too long for the class to speak in unison throughout, or where there are lines which they cannot manage very easily. It follows that the soloist in these circumstances is usually the teacher.

   In some pieces, there can be more than one soloist, provided each is competent. Indifferent speakers promote frustration.

3 **Group Speaking.** Stanzas or lines of the verse, according to the sense and effect required, are allocated to groups of speakers who say them in unison. The simplest arrangement is for the class to be divided into two, according to any convenient principle (e.g. girls and boys). In a verse of several stanzas, a number of groups may be formed and given a stanza each. Here some balancing of voices is desirable. Usually with such arrangements there is opportunity for groups to come together in unison.

   When lines or stanzas are arranged in this way, it is known as *sequential speech*. At the upper end of the junior school, use can occasionally be made of another technique in which a group of speakers, having spoken certain lines together, are joined by a second group. Later they may be joined by a third or more. This is known as *cumulative speech*. It is an effective way of building up to a climax. Conversely, and for the opposite effect, groups can be subtracted instead of added. The latter is the more difficult and it is not likely to be of much use in the junior school. An example of both sequential and cumulative group speaking is given on p. 46 where *Tiger-Lilies* is discussed. (Sequential and cumulative speech can be used by soloists instead of groups, but only perhaps when the total number of speakers is not large. In the junior school this normally implies working with only a division of the class.) Combinations of these arrangements are often possible.


## Deciding upon the Arrangement

One hesitates to suggest anything that may be taken as a rule in work of this kind, but the following may be regarded as guiding principles:—

1 Arrangements should be as simple as faithful and interesting vocal interpretation allows. If children are tied up in complicated scorings, they will inevitably lose sight of the verse.

2 Account should be taken of the ability of the children. This depends upon their experience in choral speaking as much as upon their age.

3 The arrangement should always reflect and reinforce the words of the verse; it should never be in conflict with them.

When the children are sufficiently familiar with choral speaking for them to make their own choral arrangements, they should be discouraged from spending time in discussion; it is better that they should actually try out their ideas, for this makes for the greatest involvement. It is also useful to divide the class at least into two, each section working upon a different piece.

## Deployment

Except where choral speaking is being used with mime and movement (see p. 13) any suitable deployment is acceptable. The children may even remain in their chairs if it is not convenient for them to stand, but to have them arranged in some specific fashion helps them to feel they are doing something properly. When there is division into groups, it is obviously necessary to have the speakers brought together physically, but there is no virtue in following the traditional formality of choirs, and thus soloists need not necessarily be set apart from the chorus, nor do groups need to speak in a common direction. Indeed, a perfectly satisfactory classroom arrangement is to have the children 'in the round'.

## Rhythms and Rhymes

It is normally quite beyond children (the older ones as well as the juniors) to sort out the subtleties of verse structure, let alone preserve both metrical beat and the rhythmic pattern in speaking. So difficult is this, in fact, that there are plenty of accomplished actors and actresses who cannot manage it either. When children are told to avoid hammering the metrical beat, they usually have recourse to a sing-song dirge. As verse is patterned language, there seems no good reason why in speech the pattern should not be revealed and even stressed, and it is suggested that most of the verse in WAYS selected for speaking chorally should, in fact, be spoken with its metrical stresses accentuated, and to a strict and regular beat. Thus the first two lines of *A Cat came Fiddling* (Book I, p. 4) can be spoken:

a **CAT** came **FIDD**ling **OUT** of a **BARN**, with a **PAIR** of **BAG**pipes **UND**er her **ARM**

(See also the note on p. 29 of Chapter 4).

Or the first two lines of *The Jumblies* (Book II, p. 6):

they **WENT** to **SEA** in a **SIEVE** they **DID**, in a **SIEVE** they **WENT** to **SEA**

The actual speed at which the lines are spoken must depend, of course, on mood, feeling, etc., as the content of the verse as well as its structure will suggest.

It will be seen how, when the children are able to decide these matters for themselves, they must be constantly returning to the actual verse to find the information they need about the speaking of it.

Rhymes should not present difficulties. In speech, strong rhymes appear sufficiently pointed without their receiving special attention. When therefore, the verse for speaking in chorus is strongly rhymed, as all the examples in WAYS are, the best course is to let the rhymes look after themselves.

## Refrains

Refrains, and especially those which are nonsensical, usually irritate children, for they seem to be merely an intrusion. Some teachers may like to point out that refrains were intended to be sung and that the sense of words in singing does not always have the same importance as it does in speech. They may also point out that every age has its own vocal embellishments. We have them now in pop songs; in jazz there was scat singing; in Shakespeare's day there were choruses of 'Hey Nonny', and Sir Tony Belch, in his cups, sang 'There dwelt a man in Babylon' with the refrain 'Lady! Lady!' But it is not easy to be convincing about this, because the conventions of one age do not transfer automatically to another. Except when they are an integral part of the verse structure, therefore, refrains are probably best omitted.

## Keeping Time

Without guidance, any group of inexperienced speakers has difficulty in keeping time. For this reason alone, the teacher is usually needed as conductor. In some verse where the beat of the lines is not immediately apparent or where there are irregularities (as for example in *Old King Cole*, Book I, p. 40), his presence in this role is essential. As conductor, the teacher can also, of course, help the class with such interpretative details as variation in volume.

In pieces such as *Scarecrow*, *The Roundabout* and *A Cat came Fiddling* (Book I pages 2-4 and notes on p. 29 of this book) the children can help their time-keeping by clapping and other physical action, but this also needs the teacher's overall control.

## Speaking with Music or an Effect

Speaking in time to a piece of recorded music, such as instrumental jazz, or to an effects record, such as a train, is sometimes practised by experienced groups, but it is not recommended for junior schools. The children do not have a sense of time sufficiently developed for it, and their attempts frequently end in muddle and disappointment. It will be seen that in Chapters 4 and 5 the use of recorded music and effects is sometimes suggested, but they are thought of as being incidental and supplementary to the speaking and not integrated with it.

Effects produced orally or with, for example, percussion, do not impose the same disciplines and they are recommended whenever they seem to be suitable adjuncts to the speaking of the verse. (For examples of the use of records see the notes on *Windy Nights, Engineers* and *Aeroplane* on page 30; for the use of oral and percussive effects see the notes on *The Postman* and *The Dustman* on page 30.)

## Using the Book

Once again, it depends upon the experience of the class, but generally younger children manage choral speaking better if they do not have books in their hands. (Considerable skill is required to transfer the printed word into its spoken form.) It is best, therefore, if they learn short pieces by repeating them after the teacher who, at the same time, may give some useful if incidental guidance on the actual speaking. More experienced children may approach choral speaking in the usual adult way of reading from the book. It is urged, though, that the books should be regarded as tools for the job, not as library editions, and that scorings in pencil (underlining parts, for example) should be permitted. When a verse is known, the book should be dispensed with; even when the treatment is wholly vocal, let alone when it involves action and movement (see p. 13), the book is an encumbrance. By whichever way the children approach verse for speaking chorally, the book becomes most valuable to them when the piece is known, as a comment on p. 4 explains.

# (ii) Movement and Mime

These comments are intended to supplement the notes in Chapters 4 and 5 where it is recommended that movement and mime may be used with choral speaking.

## Deployment

Where space is available, arenas rather than 'end' areas are best. They allow the children to play to any direction, which is what they do naturally. The total effect is not usually good in a visual sense, but this is not what is being sought.

## Mime

Some schools at one time illustrated verse speaking with what were termed 'actions', and the author was once given an account of how this was done with *The Burial of Sir John Moore*. When saying the first two lines

> *Not a drum was heard, not a funeral note,*
> *As his corpse to the rampart we hurried;*

the speakers were required to signify with gesture drumming, listening, blowing a bugle, and the carrying of a body. (It was not reported whether the last-named action was executed hurriedly, but presumably, in the cause of consistency, it was.) This practice was continued through the whole piece, which is eight stanzas long. The absurdity and worthlessness of such activity is obvious. It is submitted that if mime is used it must be as a reflection or a reinforcement of the verse as a whole, and not merely an illustration of certain words in it. For a piece such as *Song for a Ball-Game* (Book I, p. 58)—a particularly relevant example as it looks suited to the 'action' treatment—it is recommended that the mime consist simply of bouncing a ball in time to the beat of the verse and for the duration of the speaking. The ball might be bounced 'Underneath my right leg, And round about my knee', but there would be no representation of birds, bees, etc. or indications of the sky.

Mime and movement need care. If walking through snow, walking in the manner of a policeman, ringing a bell, drumming, etc., are to be creative activities in themselves, they must be the result of observation and thought, and in particular the size and weight of objects handled must be borne in mind. Casual movements and the vague waving of hands do little to focus attention on the verse, and as examples of mime in their own right they are useless.

## Books

It will be apparent that when mime and movement are to be used in choral speaking, nothing will be achieved when the children hold books. It is therefore expedient on most occasions to introduce any form of physical action only after the children know the verse well enough to manage without them.

# (iii) Drama and Dramatisation

## The Limitations of Verse as Material for Drama

There is not a great deal of verse that can be taught through dramatisation. Even when it contains those essential ingredients of drama, action and conflict (physical, mental or both), the economy of verse usually precludes its transference into play form. Ballads look the most promising. *The Wife of Usher's Well* (Book II, p. 30) tells a story suitable for a popular ghost play and contains passages of dialogue, but how does one act

> They hadna been a week from her,
> A week but barely ane,
> When word came to the carline wife
> That her three sons were gane.
>
> They hadna been a week from her
> A week but barely three,
> When word came to the carline wife
> That her sons she'd never see.

Even makers of films and television programmes, who are able to compress time in ways denied the stage dramatist, cannot compete with this. It is suggested that the only satisfactory way of using such material dramatically is to take the story and perhaps some scraps of the original dialogue and to make them into a wholly original dramatic work. (A note about this is given on p. 50.) The alternative of having a group of children miming while others speak the verse would seem here to be little more than illustration and on a par with 'speaking with actions' which is discussed and condemned on p. 14.

Perhaps the only piece in WAYS suitable for direct dramatisation is *The Princess and the Gipsies* (Book II, p. 27). (See note on p. 49.)

## 'Near Drama'

Terms such as 'dramatise' and 'dramatisation' are used loosely—in education and elsewhere. In a television history programme a dialogue between two characters as an alternative to straightforward exposition by a single speaker may be described as dramatisation although containing neither action nor conflict. Regarded in this sense, opportunities do arise from time to time for dramatising verse, in words or in mime. It can be termed 'near drama'. An example is *Soldier, Soldier* (Book I, p. 64) where, as the notes on p. 35 suggest, the miming of parts of the story can *expand* upon the narrative of events as told by the speakers. A greater degree of integration of speech and action is possible with *The Steeple* (Book II, p. 25). (See note on p. 49.)

Another 'near drama' approach, valuable because it obviously focuses the children's attention upon the contents of the verse, is to establish an imaginary setting for the speakers who then assume roles. In effect, they create a situation appropriate to the verse. (For an example, see the note on p. 48 about *Leave her, Johnny* (Book II, p. 22.)


## Presentation and Acting

For any kind of dramatic work, even when it is confined to the classroom, children understandably want an audience. It is helpful, therefore, to divide up the class so that when one group performs the others become spectators.

The principle of working in an arena, recommended for all choral speaking, need not be departed from—indeed, it will over-tax the skills of junior school children if they are asked to orientate their acting in one direction only—but the use of rostra and steps[1] encourages creativity and provides more visual interest for the spectators.

In dramatised verse there is little opportunity for children to characterise the parts they are playing, for the pieces are too short. In any case, characterisation is not really within their capabilities. Characterisation is not simply a matter of technique in acting, but of observation and knowledge of people, of experience of life. The most one may reasonably expect are sketches of characters, caricatures even, and generally these are good enough.


## The Shepherds

In view of the previous comment, it may be asked why the anthologists include an extract from a verse play, and one with only seven parts at that. A play was wanted so that, as a classroom project, it could be used as a climax to whatever dramatic work had been attempted with other verse; it is intended as the focal point for many kinds of creativity in costume, the dressing of the acting area, the making of properties, etc. The actual choice of *The Shepherds* was determined by the very small amount of suitable verse drama available. It is urged that it should be used only at the top end of the junior school. Full information about the play as teaching material is given in Chapter 5 on p. 50.

[1] If teachers wish to introduce special units for this purpose, they should ensure that the pieces, whilst being strong enough for all classroom use, are also light enough for the children themselves to handle. This cannot be said of all rostrum equipment which is specified as being for school use.

# (iv) Art and Craft

In Chapters 4 and 5 (pages 36 to 38, and 51 to 55), there are full notes on the teaching of individual pieces of verse through the use of art and craft. It would seem necessary here only to say what the principles of this kind of teaching are, and to add a comment or two about the more unusual kinds of equipment and materials.

## Purpose

Compared with some approaches, notably choral speaking, teaching verse through work in two and three dimensional media does not automatically produce such a thorough knowledge of the actual words and lines. But what it can do is to help children appreciate the writers' powers of observation and their ability to express experience. In other words, it teaches them to know verse without their actually learning it. The method, therefore, works towards a wider and longer term objective: the understanding of what poetry is.

## Concept

Naturally, most of the verse suitable for this approach possesses strong visual qualities. Exercises upon it fall roughly into two categories, (i) illustrative, (ii) inspirational. In the first-named there is a translation of language into some other medium of communication; work in the second category is concerned with experiences and topics *similar or allied to* those chosen by the writer. Both require close reference to the verse.

## Media

Teachers are urged to encourage work in a wide variety of media, not simply for variety's sake, but because children find many of the less usual materials exciting to use and they do not make the same technical demands on them as do painting or working in chalks and crayons, excellent as these are for children who manage them well. If modelling in clay, plasticine, etc. is too difficult for some members of the class, there are few who will not be able to contribute to the making of constructions out of scrap materials such as cardboard, and none, surely, is at a loss when it comes to collecting objects and pictures, making photo-montages from pictures in papers and magazines, or using materials for collage making. Exercises using such materials may often, of course, be carried out with the children working in pairs or in small groups.

## Children as Photographers

It will be seen that several of the notes in Chapters 4 and 5 recommend that the children should use photographs which they have taken themselves. It is suggested that all schools need a stock of simple, fixed focus, cassette loading cameras for the children to use. By about the age of seven, most children can take very passable photographs; excellent results have been obtained even by children under five. It is hard to think of a better way of encouraging observation and of stimulating a sense of composition. The snag, of course, is cost, but the cameras are not expensive, and the price of film stock is not all that much when one considers that the picture obtained can have such a wide use in the class. What is in mind here is that a class can build up a collection of its own pictures which will almost certainly be used in work other than verse.

Colour transparency is the most suitable kind of film for schools. Reasonable results are easily obtained with it, and the slides can be projected so that everybody can see them.

Where it is impossible for the children to take their own transparencies and where there is no stock in the school, teachers may obtain them from The Rickitt Encyclopedia of Slides, Portman House, 17 Brodrick Rd., London, S.W.17. When asking for lists, the subject area should be stated. The slides are sold singly and in collections. (See also the following note.)

## Other Projection Material

Using the kinds of projectors usually found in schools, highly original visual work can be stimulated with the use of home-made slides. Although some representational work can be attempted (for example by painting on small squares of glass), it is not usually successful as imperfections are magnified in projection. The best work is done by placing various transparent and translucent substances between two pieces of 3″ x 3″ ($7\frac{1}{2}$ cm. x $7\frac{1}{2}$ cm.) glass and then binding them together round the edges with adhesive tape. Materials can include grasses and pieces of foliage, jam, ash, paint, drops of oil, etc. The making of these slides is an excellent group project. The business of selecting those for use with a particular verse, as well as any eventual editing, should always, of course, be done with constant reference to the verse. The same editing process is recommended when transparency film is being used.

For suggestions on the use of these slides with *The Magnifying Glass* (Book II, p. 60), *The Flight of Birds* (Book II, p. 61), *The Banjo Player* (Book II, p. 29), and *Owl* (Book II, p. 120) see pages 54 and 55.

### The Use of Light

Some of the notes, for example those on page 37 about *The Moon* (Book I, p. 78) and *Moon Magic* (Book I, p. 80), suggest exercises using coloured light. Although the colour medium can be used with a home-made floodlight, it is simpler and safer to use a theatrical profile spotlight or fresnel spotlight on a telescopic stand. Many schools possess this equipment, but teachers requiring information should consult Rank Strand Electric Ltd., 29, King Street, Covent Garden, London, WC2E 8JH.

### Tape Recording and Tape Editing

Audial work using a tape recorder is suggested for teaching two of the poems in Book II, *Village Sounds* (p. 61) and *The Cat* (p. 106). A note on this approach may seem slightly out of place in a chapter dealing with the use of visual media, but it is as suitable a point as any in view of the growing association of sound with vision and the inclusion of these pieces in the section.

The note on p. 55 about *Village Sounds* may seem adequate but an additional word about tape editing may not perhaps be inappropriate.

It is important that there should be editing whenever tape recordings are used creatively. Unedited tapes are invariably tedious. For those unfamiliar with editing, the materials required are a tape splicing block, splicing tape, a chinagraph pencil, and a blade. Beginners are advised to make a 'rough edit' and then to refine it by re-editing. Coloured leader tape is invaluable if the tape is to be stopped and started at cues. The more sophisticated the tape recorder, the easier it is to edit; with the cheaper models where the tape cannot be quickly slipped off the playback head or the precise point of cutting the tape cannot be marked when the tape is threaded up, the job of editing is difficult.

Tape editing does not seem to be commonly undertaken by children at present, perhaps because of the risk to equipment. This is a pity as it is creative work that older juniors can manage.

# (v) Composition

### Purpose

As in the case of art and craft, the study of a piece of verse through an exercise in language leads more readily to a general appreciation and understanding of that piece than a word by word knowledge of it. The notes on page 38 and pages 56 to 60 give details of the exercises which are envisaged.

## Standards

If the exercises are to be of maximum value, the teacher should encourage precision and originality in thought and even urge that there should be selectivity. Many creative efforts by children are not as good as they could be because of the tendency of some teachers to accept, even to praise, whatever children offer. Encouragement is always necessary, and it would be a mean-spirited teacher who did not praise where praise was due, but to praise too readily is to cheapen its worth and to give children a false notion of standards. Why, after all, should they bother to do their best when they can earn approbation with less effort? (To argue thus is to assume that we work on a kind of praise or blame system, but most teachers do.) The concept of excellence for its own sake is adult, and may not always be the motive for the achievement of high standards even when it appears to be. As is pointed out elsewhere, children are unable, in the analytical sense, to be critical of other people's creative work, because they have not had the kind of experience necessary for the formation of standards, but they know well enough whether or not their own work is the best they can achieve, and teachers are not doing them any great service if they unthinkingly foster the slip-shod and the casual. It follows, of course, that the judgement of teachers in these matters rests on their knowledge of individual children, and that what can be regarded as good work by one child is poor stuff if it comes from another.

## Class and Group Work—Compiling Lists

This is a useful introductory exercise, especially as, when carried out orally, it can involve the whole class. A second step is to have groups of children working together with one of them appointed to write down the ideas on behalf of the group. The method offers plenty of opportunity for original thinking. Where experience and feelings are required, it is important to encourage those which are actual; imagination is essential in the expression of them. For examples of this approach in the hands of skilled writers, see *Shining Things* (Book I, p. 84) and *Smells* (Book II, p. 64).

## Individual Work

Other exercises, listed must inevitably be carried out individually, as follows, and since they require the written word, they all, with one exception, relate to verse contained in Book II.

### 1 Compositions conveying feeling and atmosphere

Again the work is best based upon actual experience. On the assumption that teachers will wish to deal with fact before fiction, verse suitable for use with compositions of this kind has been placed in Book II (pages 72 to 80) and precedes that which may inspire imaginative narrative writing. This, however, is a personal choice and not all will agree with it. Although it is hoped that the children will try to recall what they felt in such a situation as that described by Stevenson in *The Land of Counterpane* (Book I, p. 88), and, as the note on p. 38 suggests, relate more than simply the daily routine, they are unlikely to be able to crystallise their feelings as Stevenson does in the last stanza.

### 2 Narrative Compositions

The ultimate purpose of compositions based on verse that suggests incidents and situations instead of actually relating them (Book II, pages 81 to 85) is to draw attention to the poet's power to stimulate thought through economical writing. Generally, perhaps, this point need not be made directly; it is something which may come to the children as a later realisation.

Similarly, writing in the form of news items based on *The Ship*, *At the Railway Station*, *Upway* and *The Twa Corbies* (Book II, pages 84 to 85) helps establish the idea that verse and poetry of whatever age may have contemporary relevance.

### 3 New Viewpoints

To imagine oneself in some unusual situation physically is to see familiar things afresh. Very often it means really *seeing* them consciously for the first time, for familiarity brings, if not contempt, at least a dullness of perception. The exercise can have the same sort of effect upon children as the search for subjects and viewpoints in photography. (See page 18.) It promotes some appreciation of the poet's ability to see—which is one definition of what a poet is.

All the exercises described above are, of course, intended primarily to help in the study of particular verse, but their value as creative work in their own right cannot be overlooked.

# (vi) Original Verse

The section entitled MODELS in Book II contains nineteen pieces, most of them very short, which may encourage the children's own experiments in writing verse. There is reference to a further half-dozen or so pieces as supplementary material. Some children under the age of nine like trying their hands, but usually the skills required make it an unrealistic approach with children at the Book I stage. As always, though, it depends upon particular children. It will not be necessary, surely, to justify the writing of verse as an aid to the teaching of it. Nothing leads to understanding like doing.

## Two Approaches

Original verse writing can be approached in two ways, either through form and structure or through subject. (The skilled writer is concerned with both at the same time, of course, but with children it is wise to proceed in easy stages.) Which approach may be used initially depends upon the teacher's judgement of a particular class.

## The Form and Structure Approach

The limerick, clerihew and simple ballad stanza (alternate 3 and 4 foot lines and rhyming *a*, *b*, *c*, *b*,) are offered for the form and structure approach. They are intended, unashamedly, to be imitated, a way of learning somewhat out of favour, but not to be underestimated. The question immediately arises whether one should teach any prosody. Some explanations of metre and rhyme may seem necessary, but in most cases children who are ready to try their skills as verse writers after having worked on a good many pieces practically, especially in choral speaking, will already be aware of the patterned nature of verse, and all that is required is the drawing together of a few ends in a non-technical way. Any child with half an ear for rhythm who tries an exercise based on *My Aunt* (Book II, p. 95) should be able to see whether his efforts are technically competent, regardless of whether he knows he is using iambic feet.

One should not look for anything very weighty in content when the children are primarily concerned with structuring verse. It will be seen, of course, that all the verse offered as models for this approach may be classified as light.

## Approach through Content

When subject matter is the stimulus for metrical verse composition, it seems that the prospects of success improve in proportion to the degree of fantasy contained in the topic. In the writer's experience no work has been more successful in this respect than James Reeves' *Prefabulous Animiles*, from which

*The Osc* (Book II, p. 96), *The Doze* (Book II, p. 98) and *The Hippocrump* (Book I, p. 82) have been selected. One child of nine wrote

> The Scrimpit is a greedy beast
> Who lives on radishes and yeast

in starting a verse about a creature of his own devising, and at the time he had no technical knowledge of verse at all.

## Free Verse

Where content of a more serious nature is required, free verse is recommended. It sometimes surprises children brought up in a metrical tradition to be told that free verse is verse at all, and it is helpful if, before they write any themselves, they hear some examples read to them. Some explanation may also be necessary. (Teachers seeking information for themselves are advised to read the article "Free Verse in the Classroom" in *An Anthology of Free Verse* by James Reeves (Blackwell), but the works included in the anthology itself are mostly too difficult for junior school children.)

The notes on individual pieces on pages 62 and 63 suggest suitable exercises stemming from them, and it will be seen that a return to the 'list' exercises of the Book II section IMAGINE THAT! is recommended. Lists can often be made into acceptable free verse form, especially when the items are elaborated upon. Provided always the children have something to say—a single main idea is usually best—they invariably take readily to free verse writing, and welcome the absence of technical considerations. The following verse by a young writer, Joseph Korner, is an indication of what can be achieved:

### Growing

Small and little and does not know
about anything in the
outside world, thinking
everything is tall compared to him—
he is small with
a heavy face in place of
a big tummy. Then he sees
smaller things. He is taller
now. He thinks he is a giant
which he is to all little insects.

The writer was only eight. Of the work's many original features, perhaps none is more interesting than choice of subject. It is one which has attracted the curiosity of many a poet, John Clare, Robert Louis Stevenson and Walter de la Mare among them.

# (vii) Reading

The final section of each of the books of WAYS contains verse which does not lend itself readily to the practical methods of teaching. It appears in a book whose prime purpose is to provide verse for active use because, although personal involvement is the quickest and surest way of achieving familiarity with verse, some pieces, because of their structure or content, can only be received through the senses and/or with the intellect, and one would be sorry to deprive children of the opportunity of knowing such works as *I've got an Apple Ready* by John Walsh (Book II, p. 111) or *The Runaway* by Robert Frost (Book II, p. 129), for example. In any case, though, there are occasions when a non-practical approach is the only one available.

## Presentation

These pieces are intended to be read aloud. Most English verse is written for the voice and the ear, not the eye—at least not initially. It is desirable that first readings should normally be by the teacher; only when a child is an outstanding reader and is well prepared should the teacher relinquish this key task. First impressions are significant.

When verse is being read to them, the class simply listens—which they cannot do completely if they have their books open and are reading the words at the same time. Reading the verse for themselves is something which the children can do afterwards, or on a subsequent occasion when the piece is no longer new to them.

## When?

It is for the teacher to decide according to circumstances when the straight-forward reading of verse is to be used instead of some practical approach, but because children can listen with the necessary concentration for only a limited period, it is perhaps best to use reading as a 'fill-in'. Those odd five minutes which occur throughout the junior school week are most valuable for this. It is a positive use of time and the verse is not reduced in value if, because of the 'occasional' use it is put to, it is received and regarded as entertainment. Things entertaining can often be educational, especially at this stage.

## What?

Again, what shall be read is up to the individual teacher, but when there is time for two or three pieces, material of contrasting form and content widens the general impression of verse and obviously makes for variety. When a new verse is to be introduced, it is helpful to place it with other pieces already known to the class. This allows the new work to make its first impression with no risk of the children's confusing it with something else, which can happen when two or more new pieces are introduced at the same time.

## Explanations

See p. 5 for comments which apply to this approach as much as to any other.

## Discussion

It is virtually a tradition in education that when anything has been communicated orally, whether it be a lecture or the reading of simple verse, there must be a follow-up discussion. There is some validity in this idea if one is thinking of students or older children, but most junior school children cannot discuss anything; they simply make statements and ask questions. True, they can argue, but only when they are personally involved in an issue, and even then their cases are based on emotional responses rather than upon rationalisation. Occasionally it may be useful to hear what they have to say about the content of verse, but this will not go far beyond reporting on the story or action.

Above all, any form of critical follow-up is out of place. Criticism, in the literary sense, is based upon analysis, discrimination and taste, all of which demand an experience of life and writing which the children cannot be expected to possess. And since, for this reason, they will be unable to support their views if asked whether they like or dislike a piece, there is really no point in asking even this. In any case, their response is always apparent. In the long run, it is always best to let the verse speak for itself to the children rather than the children speak for themselves about the verse.

# 4 Teaching the Verse in Book I

*Book* 1
*Page*

## All Together

| 2 | Here we Come A-Piping | |
| 2 | Scarecrow | Eleanor Farjeon |
| 3 | The Roundabout | Clive Sansom |
| 4 | A Cat came Fiddling | |
| 4 | The Pancake | Christina Rossetti |
| 4 | December | |
| 5 | Sink Song | J. A. Lindon |
| 5 | Windy Nights | Rodney Bennett |
| 6 | Engineers | Jimmy Garthwaite |
| 7 | Aeroplane | Mary McB. Green |
| 8 | The Postman | Clive Sansom |
| 8 | The Dustman | Clive Sansom |
| 9 | The Sea Gull | Elizabeth Coatsworth |
| 9 | Sampan | |

## One and All

| 12 | Quack! | Walter de la Mare |
| 13 | Tailor | Eleanor Farjeon |
| 14 | The Owl and the Pussy-Cat | Edward Lear |
| 15 | The Clucking Hen | |
| 17 | Bats | Winifred Kingdon-Ward |
| 18 | In the Week when Christmas Comes | Eleanor Farjeon |
| 19 | Robert of Lincoln | William Cullen Bryant |
| 21 | Conjuror | Clive Sansom |
| 22 | Windy Old Weather | |

*Book* I
*Page*

23  Cowboy Spring
24  Sing a Song of Honey          Barbara Euphan Todd
26  Ho, Dandelion!               Mary Mapes Dodge
27  The King's High Drummer      Caryl Brahms
28  The Engine Driver            Clive Sansom

## Parts

30  Apple Song                   Clive Sansom
31  Dabbling in the Dew
32  Here we Come Gathering       Noel Holmes
33  Oranges and Lemons
34  Choosing Shoes               ffrida Wolfe
35  Queen Nefertiti
36  Wheelbarrow                  Eleanor Farjeon
37  Duck's Ditty                 Kenneth Grahame
38  The Band
40  Old King Cole
42  Aiken Drum
44  Slowly                       James Reeves
46  The Mysterious Cat           Vachel Lindsay

## Saying and Doing

48  Dance, Thumbkin, Dance
49  Here We Go Round the Mulberry Bush
50  Oats and Beans and Barley
52  Lachlan Gorach's Rhyme
53  Run a Little                 James Reeves
55  Mud                          Polly C. Boyden
56  There are Big Waves          Eleanor Farjeon
56  Mrs. Peck-Pigeon             Eleanor Farjeon
57  After a Bath                 Aileen Fisher
58  Song for a Ball-Game         Wilfrid Thorley
59  Skipping Song                John Walsh
61  The Sage's Pigtail           W. M. Thackeray

*Book* 1
*Page*

| | | |
|---|---|---|
| 63 | French and English | Thomas Hood |
| 64 | Soldier, Soldier | |
| 65 | The Three Singing Birds | James Reeves |

# One Thing and Another

| | | |
|---|---|---|
| 68 | Open Windows | Alexander Franklin |
| 69 | White Fields | James Stephens |
| 70 | Autumn Fires | Robert Louis Stevenson |
| 70 | Fireworks | James Reeves |
| 71 | Noah | James Reeves |
| 73 | Under the Tent of the Sky | Rowena Bennett |
| 74 | The Clown | Dorothy Aldis |
| 75 | Little Trotty Wagtail | John Clare |
| 76 | Cat | Mary B. Miller |
| 77 | The Garden Year | Sara Coleridge |
| 78 | The Song of the Year | Irene Gough |
| 78 | The Moon | Robert Louis Stevenson |
| 80 | Moon Magic | Pamela Tennant |
| 81 | Kings came Riding | Charles Williams |
| 82 | The Hippocrump | James Reeves |
| 84 | Shining Things | Elizabeth Gould |
| 86 | Noise | J. Pope |
| 87 | Boys' and Girls' Names | Eleanor Farjeon |
| 88 | The Land of Counterpane | Robert Louis Stevenson |

# Listen!

| | | |
|---|---|---|
| 90 | The King of China's Daughter | Edith Sitwell |
| 91 | Where Go the Boats? | Robert Louis Stevenson |
| 92 | Mrs. Utter | James Reeves |
| 93 | Berries | Walter de la Mare |
| 95 | Daddy Fell into the Pond | Alfred Noyes |
| 96 | Every Time I Climb a Tree | David McCord |
| 98 | Stocking and Shirt | James Reeves |
| 99 | Wynken, Blynken and Nod | Eugene Field |

*Book* 1
*Page*

| | | |
|---|---|---|
| 100 | The Month of Liverpool | |
| 101 | The Policeman | Clive Sansom |
| 102 | Block City | Robert Louis Stevenson |
| 103 | Mr. Tom Narrow | James Reeves |
| 104 | Outside | Eleanor Farjeon |
| 104 | Dachshund | Clive Sansom |
| 105 | The Knight Whose Armour Didn't Squeak | A. A. Milne |
| 108 | The Bold Piglet | 'Old Shepherd' |
| 109 | The Fairies of the Caldon Low | Mary Howitt |
| 113 | The Man in the Moon stayed up Too Late | J. R. R. Tolkien |
| 115 | Uncle John's Pig | ffrida Wolfe |
| 116 | Christmas Morning | Elizabeth Madox Roberts |

# All Together

Fourteen pieces which children enjoy saying in unison. All may be spoken with strong accentuation of the beats in the lines. (See Ch. 3 p. 11).

p. 2 **Here we Come A-Piping**
p. 2 **Scarecrow**
p. 3 **The Roundabout**
p. 4 **A Cat came Fiddling**

Lively chanting is suggested. The rhythm of a skipping rhyme will be found suitable for *Scarecrow*; it could actually be used for skipping to. Clapping on the beat of *A Cat came Fiddling* helps preserve its 'bounce', especially in 'Pipe, cat—dance, mouse' where it is best to stress each word and thus give the line the same rhythmic timing as the others. For a comment on *Here we Come A-Piping*, see Ch. 2 p. 6.

p. 4 **The Pancake**
p. 4 **December**
p. 5 **Sink Song**

With each, a mimed action may arise spontaneously or with a little encouragement. The mime for *December* is, of course, the ringing of a handbell in the manner of a town crier, and is best used to accompany the first and final lines. If *Sink Song* is too much of a tongue-twister for all the class to manage, it is worth trying it with smaller groups, or dividing the stanzas between smaller groups. (See Ch. 3 p. 14 for comments on the use of mime.)

p. 5 **Windy Nights**
p. 6 **Engineers**
p. 7 **Aeroplane**

The pieces can be supported by oral effects. To avoid the risk of the sound of wind dominating the words of *Windy Nights*, the effect can be restricted to a burst at the end; similarly the impression of machinery is sufficient after each of the two stanzas of *Engineers*. (A more sophisticated handling of this piece is described on p. 45 in a note on *Marching Song*.) The beat of *Aeroplane* is not so obvious, but it is there nevertheless. The content and form of the verse suggest variations in volume. Again, it is advisable to use appropriate effects only after the stanzas.

p. 8 **The Postman**
p. 8 **The Dustman**

The fun of doing *The Postman* is enhanced by knocking, while percussion instruments can be used to illustrate *The Dustman*.

p. 9 **The Sea Gull**
p. 9 **Sampan**

Slightly more advanced pieces in that *The Sea Gull*, unlike the other verse in the section, is not merely an impression or verbal knock-about, and *Sampan* calls for more controlled speaking. Although it admits of a variety of vocal treatments, in the present context *The Sea Gull* is best spoken as a jingle like *Here we Come A-Piping*, for example.

*Sampan*, when spoken to a slow, swinging beat, can suggest the movement of oars. Its structure indicates that from a very quiet opening, the volume should increase during the first stanza, remain constant in the second, and die away during the third.

(See also *The Moon* by Robert Louis Stevenson (Book I, p. 78), a mysterious piece if spoken slowly and in almost a whisper.)

For additional 'saying together' material see SAYING AND DOING and the notes on pp. 34 to 36.

## One and All

The verse can be spoken by a solo voice with the whole class as chorus. It is recommended for handling in this way, either because rhythm or content suggest the single voice, or because pieces are too long for unrelieved unison speaking.

It follows that the solo voice will normally be the teacher's. (For comments on the 'Soloist and Chorus' method, see Ch. 3 p. 10.)

p. 12 **Quack!**
p. 13 **Tailor**
p. 14 **The Owl and the Pussy-Cat**
p. 15 **The Clucking Hen**
p. 17 **Bats**
p. 18 **In the Week when Christmas Comes**
p. 19 **Robert of Lincoln**
p. 21 **Conjuror**
p. 22 **Windy Old Weather**
p. 23 **Cowboy Spring**

The 'joining in' parts are apparent, and the children should have little difficulty in discovering them for themselves, even in *The Clucking Hen* where the chorus role is minimal and consists only of 'clucks' and possibly the 'cock-a-doodle-do' of the last line. *Tailor* is best spoken to a regular, almost mechanical, beat throughout, and *Bats* can be treated in this way also. In the ideal, four soloists are needed for *The Owl and the Pussy-Cat* (a narrator and three characters), and vocal characterisation can hardly be on too broad or too fantastic a scale. The piece has been set to a charming tune and the children may also like singing it. (It has been recorded on Decca. Ace of Clubs. SCL 1265. *Songs from Playschool.*)

The class will like to know that *Robert of Lincoln* is about the bobolink, an American singing bird. They may also be interested to know that *Cowboy Spring* is a genuine cowboy song, and that *Windy Old Weather* is an old fisherman's song from East Anglia. Haisborough, which is mentioned in the latter's first line, is a lighthouse off the Norfolk coast, used by the fishing fleets for identifying their position, especially when returning home.

If *Quack!* proves popular and verse on a similar topic is required, teachers may like to consider *Ducks' Ditty* (Book I, p. 37). Another piece entitled *Bats* is to be found on p. 102 of Book II, but its form and content are more sophisticated.

### p. 24 Sing a Song of Honey

Suggested for solo and chorus rather than group speaking (for which it can be used) because of the variations from stanza to stanza which could make for difficulties at this stage. The parts for chorus are not immediately obvious, and it is as well for class and teacher to decide on who shall have which lines before a reading is begun. Several alternative ways of allocating lines can be found. Where the words 'is not' occur, it will be found helpful to say 'isn't'.

p. 26 **Ho, Dandelion!**
p. 27 **The King's High Drummer**
p. 28 **The Engine Driver**

Again the class can find and speak the chorus parts, but additional elements can be introduced—the blowing of a dandelion to accompany 'Whiff!' (or other blowing sound) in *Ho, Dandelion!*, a drumming action to accompany the drumming words of *The King's High Drummer*. If some of the children are sufficiently skilled, actual percussion can be used, of course, but in any event, both voice and action need to fit the underlying rhythm. In *The Engine Driver* the train rhythm is emphasised if a train effects record is played such as HMV. DFS 7006. Sound Effects, Vol. 1, but it is not advisable for young children to try speaking the piece in time to the effect. (See p. 13.) On the other hand, the onomatopaeic chorus lines may be thought sufficiently vivid without such assistance.

# Parts

Some of the pieces will be familiar to the children. They will know them as songs and may wish to sing them now. (See Ch. 2, p. 6). But their inclusion at this point is intended primarily for introducing that simple form of choral speaking in which stanzas or lines are distributed among groups of voices. At first, the teacher will probably have to decide on the composition of the groups and the allocation of the lines, but the children should be encouraged to decide these matters for themselves. (Group Speaking is discussed in Ch. 3, p. 10.) With *Here we come Gathering* and *The Band*, it is a useful extension of the work if the children make up their own additional stanzas.

p. 30 **Apple Song**
p. 31 **Dabbling in the Dew**

Division between two groups is recommended, with the addition of an 'all' chorus in *Apple Song*. In *Dabbling in the Dew* it is advisable for the group representing the girl to say the whole of the lines containing her replies; attempts to confine their parts to the direct speech with other voices saying merely 'she answered me' usually end in muddle, and even when done well, the result is scrappy. Various ideas on the handling of the last stanza are worth trying out.

p. 32 **Here we come Gathering**
p. 33 **Oranges and Lemons**
p. 34 **Choosing Shoes**
p. 35 **Queen Nefertiti**
p. 36 **Wheelbarrow**
p. 37 **Ducks' Ditty**

Content indicates that more than two groups of speakers are required with sometimes an 'all' chorus. They can sustain a different group for each stanza. With *Choosing Shoes* and *Wheelbarrow*, the teacher may need to speak with the groups to preserve the time. Both require a brisk rate, and *Choosing Shoes* has a jumpy rhythm to which the children might tap their feet.

Unless they ask, there is no need, of course, for the children to be told who Queen Nefertiti was, since the character in the verse appears to have little to do with the actual queen of Egypt.

Another choral piece about ducks which might be used with *Ducks' Ditty* is *Quack!* (Book I, p. 12).

For additional group speaking material, see *Open Windows* (Book I, p. 68) and *Kings came Riding* (Book I, p. 81).

p. 38 **The Band**
p. 40 **Old King Cole**
p. 42 **Aiken Drum**

In each, a group or groups can supply sounds. Perhaps in *The Band* the 'instrumentalists' might take the whole of a stanza a-piece. In *Old King Cole* the structure suggests that the groups specialise, as it were, in their effects lines only, leaving all other children to speak the rest of the verse. In *Aiken Drum*, groups might speak the stanzas with everybody saying the choruses. The latter can be accompanied by a small group of actual instruments (e.g. drum, recorder, mouth organ, ladle and tin can) or by suitable sounds produced orally.

In all three pieces, it is advisable for a strict, regular beat to be maintained. The rhythm of *Old King Cole* is the most difficult to preserve, and, each time, after 'Twee, tweedle dee, tweedle dee, went the fiddlers' it is best to have two silent beats before going on to the chorus. This invariably means that the teacher must conduct. (See Ch. 3, p. 12. 'Keeping Time' for comments on the use of a conductor.)

(A similar approach is suggested on p. 45 for *The Ceremonial Band* (Book II, p. 10), which is a more difficult piece.)

p. 44 **Slowly**
p. 46 **The Mysterious Cat**

These reward more complex group arrangements. One line per group and a final chorus suggests itself for *Slowly*; a cumulative arrangement (see p. 10) for *The Mysterious Cat*. Both pieces, it is suggested, should be spoken slowly and quietly.

For additional group speaking material see SAYING AND DOING and the notes on pp. 34 to 36.

# Saying and Doing

A variety of speaking arrangements can be used, such as 'saying together' and 'group speaking', but the selection has been made with mime, movement and even rudimentary acting in mind. Such activities require floor space. When it is not available, many of the pieces can be used for voices only.

p. 48 **Dance, Thumbkin, Dance**
p. 49 **Here We Go Round the Mulberry Bush**
p. 50 **Oats and Beans and Barley**

If these are considered too elementary, teachers will not, of course, use them, since little is gained when children work on material which they consider babyish. Nevertheless, many song and rhyme games are enjoyed by children long after the nursery and infant stages. (*Here We Go Round the Mulberry Bush*, for example, is known in numerous versions, but this does not preclude its use by children as an exercise in oral composition. Experience shows that the youngest schoolchildren can extend it almost indefinitely.) These oral classics are too well-known to require notes on their treatment, but teachers wishing for information about variations, tunes, or requiring other rhymes, are referred to such works as *The Oxford Dictionary of Nursery Rhymes* and *The Lore and Language of Schoolchildren* by I. & P. Opie (Oxford), *The Traditional Games of England, Scotland and Ireland* by Alice Bertha Gomme (Dover Publications Inc. N.Y.) and *The Children's Song Book* by Elizabeth Poston (Bodley Head).

p. 52 **Lachlan Gorach's Rhyme**
p. 53 **Run a Little**

Nothing more elaborate than straightforward chanting is needed as the children dance and/or clap in time to the words of *Lachlan Gorach's Rhyme* or carry out in mime and movement the clear directions of *Run a Little*.

p. 55 **Mud**
p. 56 **There are Big Waves**
p. 56 **Mrs. Peck-Pigeon**
p. 57 **After a Bath**
p. 58 **Song for a Ball-Game**

Recommended for saying together in chorus while miming. None requires particular concentration on the tonal quality of the speech or on its arrangement. Action, whether it is walking through imaginary mud, miming waves, the movement of pigeons, towelling, or bouncing a ball, needs to be a reflection of the verse and not merely an illustration of it. (See Ch. 3, p. 14 for comments on mime and action as an accompaniment to verse as opposed to the outmoded practice of speaking with actions.)

p. 59 **Skipping Song** ⎱
p. 61 **The Sage's Pigtail** ⎬
p. 63 **French and English** ⎰

Group arrangements are best for the speech. To speak *Skipping Song* to a 'skipping' beat means stressing thus:

> when **BREAD**-and-**CHEESE**
> on **HAW**thorn **TREES**
> make **BUDS** of **TI**ny **GREEN**;
> when **BIG** dogs **CHASE**
> a**ROUND** and **LIT**tle
> **DOGS** run **IN** be**TWEEN** . . . .

All three can be reinforced with mime and movement. Skipping (mimed or with actual ropes) might be restricted to accompanying the chorus lines of *Skipping Song*. To say *The Sage's Pigtail* can be an amusing experience for the children if they turn and twist as the verse indicates, especially if they devise and wear pigtails made of wool. (If the numbers are large, half the class can perform it to the other, and perhaps stand in well-spaced columns to avoid mishap.) It is suggested that the comic situations described in *French and English* should not be attempted during the speaking, but as a wholly separate exercise afterwards on communication by signs and mime. Another look at the verse following these efforts will enhance its value, for, lighthearted as it is, it is not without point.

## p. 64 **Soldier, Soldier**

Various ways of using this piece include singing and speaking it in groups— one group for the maid's lines, one for the soldier's, and a third (or the whole class) for the narrative parts. It is placed here, however, because it can be used in a 'near dramatic' manner. (See Ch. 3, p. 15 for an explanation of 'Near Drama'.) In this case, the roles of the maid and the soldier need to be mimed by the soloists as well as spoken by them. Ideally, their performance should end with the response of the maid to the soldier's announcement that he is married, and perhaps his attempt to escape with his ill-gotten gains. The rest of the class can speak the narration in chorus, or some of them may be able to make an oral drumming accompaniment and to mime drumming. In any speaking version, the preservation of a regular, drumming rhythm is recom- mended. (A further piece for similar 'drumming'—but with no dramatisation— is *Marching Song* (Book II, p. 5.) (See note on p. 45.)

## p. 65 **The Three Singing Birds**

A charming narrative piece which allows group speaking as simple or as complex as desired or thought attainable. So vivid a story immediately suggests some kind of dramatisation, but, as is pointed out in Ch. 3, even verse in ballad form seldom permits its story to be acted satisfactorily while the words

35

are spoken. In another context, one can imagine a ballet on this theme. In the junior school, the piece could be the basis of a mime or dance/mime to which an original accompaniment of mysterious sounds could be made up, using school instruments. The king, the maid, and the three birds are the essential roles, but many other children could take part as courtiers and members of the palace household, and at the end, in the tradition of ballet, there might be a wedding dance in which even the rank and file citizens could join.

The story told in *Mr. Tom Narrow* (Book I, p. 103) may be found suitable for a dramatic improvisation. (See note on p. 39 of this book.)

## One Thing and Another

These pieces are grouped together because they can be taught through creative work in visual media or in words. Usually, the verse will be the starting point, but occasionally it may be thought best to introduce it after ancillary exercises have been completed. The value of both verse and creative work need not be affected because they are used complementarily; indeed, with careful selection, both may be enhanced. (For comments on the use of creative work in the teaching of verse, see Ch. 3, pp. 17 and 19.) Some pieces listed in this section can be taught in other ways, for example, *The Moon* may be spoken in unison, and *Open Windows* and *Kings came Riding* with groups and chorus. (See notes on pp. 30 and 33.)

p. 68 **Open Windows**
p. 69 **White Fields**
p. 70 **Autumn Fires**
p. 70 **Fireworks**
p. 71 **Noah**
p. 73 **Under the Tent of the Sky**
p. 74 **The Clown**
p. 75 **Little Trotty Wagtail**

Straightforward illustrating should not be undervalued, for it requires constant reference to the verse; on the other hand, inspiration gained from considering a piece and then working visually on a *similar or allied* topic encourages children to look at things with something of the eye of poets and artists. Paint, chalk and crayon may still be the most popular media and especially suitable perhaps for depicting the three aspects of Noah, animal-clouds, or some composite illustration of the life and ways of the wagtail or any other bird, information about such common birds as the starling and the sparrow being easily obtainable simply by observing—a most valuable exercise in this context. But other media are sometimes more appropriate; collage is particularly suited to exercises based on *White Fields* (where white and silver materials might be used), *Autumn Fires, Fireworks* and *The Clown*. The last four lines of the latter suggest something more than the merely representational.

Many other pieces in this book are, of course, suitable for use with visual exercises, especially perhaps *The Roundabout* (p. 3), *Ducks' Ditty* (p. 37)—another good subject for collage—*The Three Singing Birds* (p. 65).

p. 76 **Cat**
p. 77 **The Garden Year**
p. 78 **The Song of the Year**

A trio which may promote the selection of pictures reflecting or reinforcing the contents of the verse. The various postures and movements of cats should not present difficulties. Newspapers and magazines are the likeliest sources, though some children may try taking their own photographs; colour transparency photography, in particular, is well within the capabilities of many children even younger than seven, (see Ch. 3, p. 18). (A further piece about cats suitable at this stage only for reading to the children is *Catalogue* (Book II, p. 54). *The Garden Year* and *The Song of the Year* (which is about Australia) are included as complementary pieces and are thought of as being used together. Illustrations of the months in Britain may not be hard to come by, especially if the children do not confine their choice to the rural scene, but also include pictures of urban life. The Australian year is, of course, another matter, and where material is short some home-produced, imaginative illustrations are a fair substitute.

p. 78 **The Moon**
p. 80 **Moon Magic**

It will almost certainly be beyond the capabilities of the children to capture the feeling of these pieces in their own visual work. It is suggested that they make models from scraps, or in modelling clay or plasticine, or paint pictures, etc. of suitable subjects such as landscapes, and then see what the effect is when they are flooded with 'moonlight', ie. electric light with a Steel (No. 17) colour medium placed in front of it. (Cinemoid, suitable for this use, is obtainable from Rank Strand Electric, 29 King Street, Covent Garden, London, WC2E 8JH. Unison speaking of *The Moon* might be used in conjunction with the lighting effect.

p. 81 **Kings came Riding**
p. 82 **The Hippocrump**

The making of a model showing one of the situations described in *Kings came Riding* is a stimulating way of focusing attention on the verse. Scrap materials, modelling clay or plasticine can be used. If this is not possible, the vivid verbal colours of the verse may be translated into a painting.

37

*The Hippocrump* has almost universal appeal. Children as young as five receive it enthusiastically, despite their not understanding many of the words; adults appreciate in particular such features as the satirical echo of a hymn in the last line. It could have been placed in either book of the series, but it appears here, partly because its pleasures should not be withheld longer than necessary, and partly because, at this point, it can make a valuable contribution to visual creative work.

The representation of a monster (either the Hippocrump or some other fantastic beast) need not necessarily be two-dimensional. Materials such as cardboard boxes allow constructions approaching 'life' size to be undertaken as a group or class activity.

Another piece which can promote the making of a large structure is *Scarecrow* (Book I, p. 2).

p. 84 **Shining Things**
p. 86 **Noise**
p. 87 **Boys' and Girls' Names**
p. 88 **The Land of Counterpane**

Four pieces which can stimulate ideas and expression in words. If the children's writing is slow and likely to be inhibiting, individual or group oral work may be preferable. *Shining Things, Noise* and *Boys' and Girls' Names* are lists. The children can make up their own lists of shining (or dull) things, and their own favourite (or most hated) noises. A list based on *Boys' and Girls' Names* takes inventiveness a stage further if, after the manner of Eleanor Farjeon, similies are found as well as names. (Further inspiration for list-making may be provided by *Slowly*, Book I, p. 44.) Actual prose composition can stem from *The Land of Counterpane*. A day or two in bed is within every child's experience, but if Stevenson's example is to be followed, the writing needs to be more than an account of the daily routine. (For discussion on the possibilities of children's creative work in words, see Ch. 3, p. 20.)

Other prose composition exercises can be based on *Daddy Fell into the Pond* (p. 95), *Every Time I Climb a Tree* (p. 96), and *Uncle John's Pig* (p. 115).

As is suggested on pp. 32-34 of these notes, original verse composition can be based on *Here we Come Gathering* (Book I, p. 32), *The Band* (Book I, p. 38), and *Here we go Round the Mulberry Bush* (Book I, p. 49).

# Listen!

This final section consists of verse which can be read to the class by the teacher. There is a variety of forms, standards of difficulty and subject matter, and it is anticipated that there will normally be selection, but if it is preferred to read in sequence, the order in which the pieces have been arranged will automatically provide this variety. What shall be read, who shall read it, and when it shall be read are questions for the teacher to decide, but some views on these matters are expressed in Ch. 3 on p. 24. Also dealt with there is the question of what kind of comment, if any, might follow a reading.

p. 90 **The King of China's Daughter**

p. 91 **Where Go the Boats?**

p. 92 **Mrs. Utter**

p. 93 **Berries**

It may be as well to make sure by question and answer that all the children know why the old woman found such a bumper crop and why she hid the small, extra pot 'A good thumb deep, Half way over from Wicking to Weep.'

*pottle* (*l.*5) is almost certainly used here to mean a small fruit basket.

p. 95 **Daddy Fell into the Pond**
p. 96 **Every Time I Climb a Tree**

Both may also be used as a basis for composition. (See note on *The Land of Counterpane* on p. 38.)

p. 98 **Stocking and Shirt**

p. 99 **Wynken, Blynken and Nod**

p. 100 **The Month of Liverpool**

p. 101 **The Policeman**

*The Policeman* (Book II, p. 110) might sometimes be suitable as a complementary piece.

p. 102 **Block City**

p. 103 **Mr. Tom Narrow**

The story could be used for an improvised scene, with dialogue comprising quotations from the piece as well as wholly original utterances. It is hardly possible, however, for a dramatisation to take place while the verse is spoken.

p. 104 **Outside**

p. 104 **Dachshund**
        To encourage imaginative listening, it is suggested that the children have their books closed and that the pieces are read to them without their titles. After *Outside* they guess the identity of the speaker; after *Dachshund* they say what kind of a dog is described.

p. 105 **The Knight Whose Armour Didn't Squeak**

p. 108 **The Bold Piglet**
        The author, 'Old Shepherd', was a west-country folk singer who lived from about 1815 to about 1903. If the dialect is not required, the piece can easily be adapted into Standard English and the grammar modified.

        a *tallat* (*l*.5) is a meal-loft reached by an outside ladder.
        a *barton* (*l*.11) is a cowshed.

p. 109 **The Fairies of the Caldon Low**

p. 113 **The Man in the Moon stayed up Too Late**

p. 115 **Uncle John's Pig**
        May also be used as a basis for composition. (See note on *The Land of Counterpane on* p. 38.)

p. 116 **Christmas Morning**

# 5 Teaching the Verse in Book II

*Book II*        **Many Voices**
*Page*

| 2 | A Piper | Seumas O'Sullivan |
| 2 | The Fifteen Acres | James Stephens |
| 5 | Marching Song | Thomas Hardy |
| 5 | The Main-Deep | James Stephens |
| 6 | The Jumblies | Edward Lear |
| 9 | The Toy Band: A Tale of the Great Retreat | Sir Henry Newbolt |
| 10 | The Ceremonial Band | James Reeves |
| 12 | Old Zip Coon | David Stevens |
| 13 | An Indian Summer on the Prairie | Vachel Lindsay |
| 14 | The Dancing Cabman | J. B. Morton |
| 15 | The Tide Rises, The Tide Falls | Henry Wadsworth Longfellow |
| 15 | Christmas Everywhere | Phillips Brooks |
| 16 | Tiger-Lilies | Thomas Bailey Aldrich |
| 17 | The Gipsy Laddie | |
| 19 | The Ballad of Semmerwater | William Watson |
| 20 | The Piper O' Dundee | |
| 21 | Oliver Cromwell | |
| 22 | Leave her, Johnny | |
| 23 | The Whale | |
| 24 | Hunting Song | |
| 25 | The Steeple | Elizabeth Fleming |
| 27 | The Princess and the Gipsies | Frances Cornford |
| 29 | The Banjo Player | Clifford Dyment |
| 30 | The Wife of Usher's Well | |
| 32 | The Shepherds | Alexander Franklin (adapter) |

# Hand and Eye

42 Granton — Norman MacCaig
43 The Smuggler
44 A Ship sails up to Bideford — Herbert Asquith
45 'The General Elliott' — Robert Graves
46 The Painting — Oscar Wilde
47 Song — Richard Watson Dixon
47 Old Dan'l — L. A. G. Strong
48 The Arrival — John Walsh
49 On these November Evenings — John Walsh
51 November Morning — Olive Dehn
52 A Sheep Fair — Thomas Hardy
54 Catalogue — Rosalie Moore
55 August Weather — Katharine Tynan
56 Thrushes — Humbert Wolfe
56 London to Paris by Air — Lord Ronald Gorell
58 Water Picture — May Swenson
59 The Shining Streets of London — Alfred Noyes
60 Tugs — George Rostrevor Hamilton
60 The Magnifying Glass — Walter de la Mare
61 The Flight of Birds — John Clare
61 Village Sounds — James Reeves

# Imagine That!

64 Smells — Christopher Morley
65 Names for Twins — Alastair Reed
67 What is Grey? — Mary O'Neill
68 What is White? — Mary O'Neill
69 Digging — Edward Thomas
70 Fairy Things — John Clare
71 The Wood-Cutter's Night Song — John Clare
72 November — John Clare
73 Hay Harvest — Patrick R. Chalmers
74 Down with the Holly, Ivy, All . . . — Robert Herrick
74 Peter to Tea — John Walsh
76 The New Boy — John Walsh
77 Anne and the Field-Mouse — Ian Serraillier
78 The Rescue — Hal Summers

*Book II*
*Page*

| | | |
|---|---|---|
| 80 | At the Theatre | A. P. Herbert |
| 81 | The Apple Tree | James Stephens |
| 83 | The Fugitive | Dorothy Margaret Stuart |
| 84 | My Bonny Lad | |
| 84 | The Ship | J. C. Squire |
| 85 | At the Railway Station, Upway | Thomas Hardy |
| 85 | The Twa Corbies | |
| 86 | The Snail | John Gay |
| 86 | The Lonely Scarecrow | James Kirkup |
| 87 | On a Cat, Ageing | Alexander Gray |
| 87 | The Fly | Walter de la Mare |
| 88 | Under Ground | James Reeves |
| 89 | The Dumb Soldier | Robert Louis Stevenson |

# Models

| | | |
|---|---|---|
| 92 | There was an Old Man with a Beard | Edward Lear |
| 92 | There was an Old Man in a Barge | Edward Lear |
| 92 | There was an Old Man of Peru | |
| 93 | Obvious Reasons | Lewis Carroll |
| 93 | There was a Young Lady of Sheen | |
| 93 | A Cheerful Old Bear at the Zoo | |
| 94 | Kindness to Animals | Laura Richards |
| 95 | Dr. W. G. Grace | E. C. Bentley |
| 95 | My Aunt | |
| 96 | The Osc | James Reeves |
| 98 | The Doze | James Reeves |
| 99 | The Marrog | R. C. Scriven |
| 100 | The Horny-Goloch | |
| 100 | Fog | Carl Sandburg |
| 100 | Wind and Silver | Amy Lowell |
| 101 | The Runner | Walt Whitman |
| 101 | Roses | George Eliot |
| 101 | Gale Warning | Michael Roberts |
| 102 | Bats | Randall Jarrell |

# Listen Again!

| | | |
|---|---|---|
| 104 | Please to Remember | Walter de la Mare |
| 105 | Marjorie Sitting on the Doorstep | John Walsh |
| 106 | The Cat | Richard Church |

*Page*
*Book II*

| | | |
|---|---|---|
| 107 | Out at Night | John Walsh |
| 108 | The Quangle Wangle's Hat | Edward Lear |
| 110 | The Policeman | Jan Struther |
| 111 | I've Got an Apple Ready | John Walsh |
| 112 | Wonders of Modern Science | |
| 112 | Conkers | Clive Sansom |
| 114 | Sweet Chestnuts | John Walsh |
| 115 | A Visit from the Sea | Robert Louis Stevenson |
| 116 | A Spike of Green | Barbara Baker |
| 116 | The Helicopter | Ian Serraillier |
| 117 | The Bat | Theodore Roethke |
| 117 | Moonlit Apples | John Drinkwater |
| 118 | Priest's Hole | Gregory Harrison |
| 119 | The Snake | Emily Dickinson |
| 120 | Owl | Randall Jarrell |
| 120 | Cuckoos | Andrew Young |
| 121 | The Hens | Elizabeth Madox Roberts |
| 123 | Martha of Bethany | Clive Sanson |
| 124 | The Fog | W. H. Davies |
| 125 | In Spring-Time | W. H. Davies |
| 126 | Target Area | Peter Roberts |
| 127 | Cock-Crow | Edward Thomas |
| 128 | Something Told the Wild Geese | Rachel Field |
| 129 | The Runaway | Robert Frost |
| 129 | The Ballad of Billy Rose | Leslie Norris |
| 132 | The Oxen | Thomas Hardy |

# Many Voices

All the verse is for more than one speaker. The pieces are grouped according to their suggested use—unison speaking, solo and chorus, group speaking, with movement, for dramatisation, etc. (See Ch. 3 for discussion on the principal approaches to choral speaking in the junior school.) There is also an extract from a verse play.

### p. 2 **A Piper**

Recommended for unison speaking on a lively, regular beat reinforced, perhaps, with clapping. (For use with dance see p. 48.)

### p. 2 **The Fifteen Acres**

Used for the whole class to speak together, it is best tackled with the children 'backing' a strong solo lead provided by the teacher. It can be spoken 'on the

44

beat', but needs to be said more slowly than *A Piper* and with a swinging rhythm.

### p. 5 **Marching Song**

The speakers might mark time to the strong, iambic beat. Although straightforward unison speaking is satisfactory, there is added interest if a small group provides a drumming accompaniment with either actual percussion or by repeating over and over some onomatopœic phrase such as **RUM**-ta-ta-**TUM-TUM**. The easiest way of handling the refrain is:

'Right (*pause one beat*) fol-lol!'

A visual feature can be introduced by having the speakers in the form of a military column.

(If this kind of two-part arrangement proves popular and more material is needed, see *Soldier, Soldier* (Book I, p. 64) and the note on p. 35 of this book.

It is also possible to use *Engineers* (Book I, p. 6) by having the main body of the class speak the words in unison while a second and smaller group stress the beat of the line with machinery effects.)

### p. 5 **The Main-Deep**

This requires slow, controlled speaking, with a lengthening of the sounds the poet has indicated with accents. To speak the verse over a recording of sea music such as *The Hebridean Overture* by Mendelssohn heightens the impression of the sea in motion. The piece is best suited to older children.

### p. 6 **The Jumblies**

A simple solo and chorus speaking is adequate, but various character parts can be found, if desired. A further example of Edward Lear's poetic nonsense is *The Owl and the Pussy-Cat* (Book I, p. 14) with note on p. 31 of this book.

### p. 9 **The Toy Band: A Tale of the Great Retreat**

A few lines spoken aloud will reveal how strong an impression of drumming they contain—so strong, indeed, that perhaps it will be thought inappropriate to use the accompaniment of a real drum. It is suggested that this regular, drumming rhythm can be maintained throughout the speaking of the piece. An arrangement for soloist and chorus is the most suitable, although variations can be introduced.

### p. 10 **The Ceremonial Band**

The whole class can say it together, with solo voices for the instrument lines. It should be spoken to a firm and steady beat to convey the impression of the orchestra playing. If the last line is said with plenty of volume and the rate slowed a little, there will be a suggestion that the musicians are playing a piece in the style of Bach or Handel.

A similar approach is recommended on p. 33 for *The Band* (Book I, p. 38) and *Old King Cole* (Book I, p. 40.).

p. 12 **Old Zip Coon**

The principal speaker should be the teacher if the rather difficult rhythm and bouncy beat are to be maintained. Percussion or clapping could be used as an accompaniment to the choruses, where the whole class joins in.

p. 13 **An Indian Summer on the Prairie**

It is suggested that there should be different groups for the second, third and fourth stanzas, with the first stanza divided between them. The moods need to be reflected in the rate and volume of the speech. The 'headings' may be omitted, or spoken by a solo voice.

p. 14 **The Dancing Cabman**

A satisfactory arrangement is for a large group to take stanzas 1, 3 and 5, with a small group for stanzas 2 and 4. Clearly, a dancing beat should be maintained throughout; in the first stanza it can be achieved if stressed thus:

> aLONE on the **LAWN**
> the **CAB**man **DAN**ces;
> in the dew of **DAWN**
> he **KICKS** and **PRAN**ces.

p. 15 **The Tide Rises, The Tide Falls**

Various group arrangements are possible. The following might be acceptable for the first stanza:

> *Group* 1: The tide rises,
> *Group* 2: the tide falls,
> *Group* 1: The twilight darkens,
> *Group* 2: the curlew calls;
> *All*:  Along the sea-sands damp and brown
>  The traveller hastens toward the town,
> *Solo*:  And the tide rises, the tide falls.

The use of a solo voice for the last line of each stanza should reinforce the feeling of mystery. The whole piece might be spoken slowly and quietly.

p. 15 **Christmas, Everywhere**

There can be parts for soloists and/or groups of speakers, and a chorus for everybody. The children themselves should find it fairly easy to suggest the division.

p. 16 **Tiger-Lilies**

The overall structure and the straightforwardness of the lines suggest both sequential and cumulative group speaking. (See Ch. 3, p. 10.) If the class is divided into three, for example, the first stanza might be arranged thus:

| | |
|---|---|
| *Group* 1: | I like not lady-slipper, |
| *Group* 2: | Nor yet the sweet-pea blossoms, |
| *Group* 3: | Nor yet the flaky roses, |
| | Red, or white as snow; |
| *Group* 1: | I like the chaliced lilies, |
| *Groups* 1 *and* 2: | The heavy Eastern lilies, |
| *Groups* 1, 2 *and* 3: | The gorgeous tiger-lilies, |
| | That in our garden grow. |

The sense of the second and third stanzas indicates that they can be spoken in similiar, but not identical ways.

### p. 17 The Gipsy Laddie

One of many versions of a popular folk tale. Most of it can be spoken by groups, or even the whole class, but soloists would seem necessary for the squire (stanza 2), his lady (stanzas 5 and 9), and perhaps the servant's line in stanza 1. Stanzas 4 and 6 are not recommended for soloist; they are in a kind of indirect speech and too many solo lines will spoil the balance of the whole piece.

The refrain is probably best used twice, as printed, although it is meant to follow each stanza when sung. (See Ch. 3, p. 12 on refrains.) On the final chorus, it might be found pleasing to have the line 'She's gone with the gypsum Davy' repeated *ad lib* and 'faded out'.

*The Gipsy Laddie* is insufficiently dramatic in structure for acting. Vocal characterisation is the nearest one can get to dramatisation.

A modern variation which may be considered is *The Princess and the Gipsies* (Book II, p. 27), and this, as the notes on p. 49 indicate, may be used for drama.

Both can be used for imaginative writing. (See also note on p. 59, *My Bonny Lad.*)

### p. 19 The Ballad of Semmerwater

An atmospheric piece for measured speaking by a variety of voices—solo, groups, the whole class. Obviously, much of it needs to be said quietly, and the effect of mystery and remoteness can be reinforced if a record such as Debussy's *Cathedral Under the Sea* is played as a backing to the speech.

an *eller* (stanza 5) is a herdsman.

(See also p. 52 for a note on visual work.)

The remainder of the verse in this section is recommended for physical as well as vocal approaches.

### p. 20 The Piper O' Dundee

Spoken to a regular dance beat, it may inspire improvised dance steps. If all the speakers dance, group arrangements are probably advisable so that nobody has to do too much speaking and dancing at the same time. The refrain (spoken by all perhaps) can be used after each stanza. If the Scottish names and tune titles are too difficult, the piece could be reduced to the first stanza and refrain only.

*Aiken Drum* (Book I, p. 42) and *A Piper* (Book II, p. 2) can be used in the same way.

### p. 21 Oliver Cromwell

A group and chorus arrangement is easily devised, and interest can be increased if the speakers stand as if round a grave and two of the class mime Oliver Cromwell and the old woman. The children may like to know that the strange events described are an expression of an old superstition that someone who gathered fruit from a tree planted on a grave gained power over the soul of the dead person. But it was also believed that the ghost of the deceased could rise to prevent the fruit from being taken.

*Oliver Cromwell* (also called *Old Roger, Sir Roger*, etc.) is a traditional singing game. It is described fully in Vol. II of *Traditional Games of England, Scotland and Ireland* by Alice B. Gomme (Dover Publications Inc. N.Y.).

### p. 22 Leave her, Johnny

A capstan or windlass shanty. It would not be too unfaithful a representation of one of its original uses if the children, in the role of sailors, did a mime in which they push round the bars of a capstan. With not too much concern for the authentic timing of the action, they could speak the chorus line as they went round, while one of their number—placed apart—spoke the verses as shantyman or official song leader. Alternatively, they could sing the words as, of course, seamen did. The tune can be found in *Something to Sing*, edited by Geoffrey Brace (Cambridge University Press).

*wear* and *stay* (Stanzas 3 and 4). A sailing ship makes headway against the wind by tacking, i.e. sailing a series of zig-zag courses. The usual way of changing from one tack to another is to do so with the ship heading up into the wind. She *stays* if she remains successfully on a tack or can be shifted from one to another. If the ship *wears* she takes up a new tack only by going round with her stern to the wind, a clumsy manoeuvre which, in some conditions, is all a ship can be made to do. As the ship in the song would neither wear nor stay, she was thoroughly bad.

*shipped it green* (stanza 3). The ship was flooded by waves which broke over her deck.

*take a run* (stanza 5). A spell of shore leave.

### p. 23 The Whale

The class might be arranged in a 'deck' setting. The lines could be spoken by a series of soloists, with everybody joining in the chorus, to suggest sailors yarning. (See Ch. 3, p. 15 for comments on the use of 'Near Drama.') If it is preferred to sing *The Whale*, the tune can be found in *The Burl Ives Song Book* (Ballantine Books).

'*on your davit tackles fall*' (stanza 4) is the captain's order for the boats to be lowered. A *davit* (pronounced by seamen *day-vit*) is a crane-like arm on the deck for lowering a boat into the water and for hoisting it back on board. There are normally two davits to each boat. *Tackle* (pronounced by seamen *tay-kle*) is a set of pulley blocks and rope. The davit tackle is attached at one end to the davit and at the other hooked on to the boat.

(See note on p. 52 for using this piece in a painting exercise.)

## p. 24 Hunting Song

A variety of speech arrangements are possible, but different groups with perhaps the first and final stanzas as choruses make for the greatest involvement. The class may be able to suggest a suitable setting, such as a tavern gathering, in which the vigour of the lines (and the speech) would be appropriate.

## p. 25 The Steeple

An arrangement for groups of speakers and chorus is suggested. At the same time, the children might attempt a dramatic impression of the event. They could be villagers admiring the steeple in stanza 1, reacting to a blizzard in stanzas 2, 3 and 4, showing feelings after a storm in 5 and 6, and, in the final three stanzas, become straightforward narrators.

## p. 27 The Princess and the Gipsies

Compared with all preceding verse, *The Princess and the Gipsies* affords the most opportunities for orthodox dramatisation. It could be spoken entirely by soloists who act the meeting; on the other hand, the gipsies might speak in small groups. In either event, though, where the princess merely relates her experiences (i.e. in the first two and the last two stanzas), she is best advised to become a narrator, albeit in character. The dramatisation is thin if it is confined wholly to the situations of the verse; visual interest in the form of, for example, the princess's life at court and the gipsies at work, can supplement it to good effect. Varying acting levels help the action, but are not essential. (See Ch. 3, p. 16).

The contrast between this story and that of *The Gipsy Laddie* (Book II, p. 17 and notes on p. 47 of this book) may provide a talking point. Both can be used for imaginative writing (see notes on p. 59 and p. 61.)

## p. 29 The Banjo Player

The arrangement of the piece for speaking is unimportant as a basis for dramatic work; it can be spoken in unison, in groups, or by a soloist. What matters most, it is suggested, is that something of the poet's power of observation and his imagination should be captured in two improvised scenes to be acted in their own right, not as an accompaniment to the verse. The scenes, which need contain no actual story, should be complementary and contrasting, as they are in *The Banjo Player*. They need not, of course, be the same as those related by the poet; any suitable situation shown under contrasting conditions, such as hot and cold, should focus attention on the verse. The piece can also be taught through art work and there is a note about it on p. 55.

## p. 30 The Wife of Usher's Well

A magnificent, traditional ballad, but too difficult perhaps for all but the oldest children. Its story is dramatic, even theatrical, but, in the nature of ballads, it is potential rather than actual dramatic material. To enact the situations as the verse is spoken is to illustrate merely, and, with such swift changes of scene and mood, even this can hardly be adequate. It is suggested that the piece should be used as a basis for a dramatic improvisation in which, if some of the original lines are used, the majority are new. It might start with the rich, old wife recounting to members of her household how her three sons had gone abroad and how she had received news that they were dead. Their appearance and her reaction can follow closely the story of the ballad, though added to this might be an episode of rejoicing. This leads logically to the household's retiring to sleep and then the sound of the cock crowing. The scene ends with the sons' departure and the still-sleeping figure of the wife, suggesting the anguish to follow; or perhaps some children will wish to show her discovering they have gone and her subsequent reaction. Depending upon the ability of the children, various subtleties can be introduced, such as a member of the household suspecting that the men are ghosts, or the youngest son being in love with the serving lass 'that kindles my mother's fire'. There is, though, little likelihood of their being able to handle the complexities of the wife's character which the verse suggests, or conveying the dark, brooding atmosphere. As a means to bringing familiarity with the verse, these refinements do not matter much, however.

For purely choral speaking, which may be a good way of introducing the poem, an arrangement for groups and soloists suggests itself.

The ballad can be anglicised for speaking, but it then loses some of the power contained in the Scottish. The following is a glossary of the more difficult words:

*carline* (stanza 2): ancient  
*fashes* (stanza 4): turbulences  
*mirk* (stanza 5): dark  
*birk* (stanza 5): birch. (Hats made of birch were thought to be a charm against evil spirits.)

*syke* (stanza 6): marsh  
*sheugh* (stanza 6): trench  
*channering* (stanza 13): fretting  

## p. 32 The Shepherds

This passage from a miracle play rewards performance. Reading in parts is preferable to no live performance at all, but even this is very much second best.

It should perhaps be explained to the class that in many towns and villages in the 14th, 15th and 16th centuries, religious plays were acted on platforms in the streets. *The Shepherds* is one of these plays and was acted in Chester at Whitsun. They may also like to know that the reason the shepherds cannot understand the angel is that, being simple men, they do not understand Latin—the language of the Bible and the church services in those days, and therefore thought to be the language of heaven.

*Characters* Hankin—the natural leader
Sym—ragged and henpecked
Tud—elderly
Trowle—young, down-to-earth
The Angel
Mary
Joseph—an old man (in the miracle play tradition)

It is suggested that, for a variety of reasons including regard for the spirit of medieval drama, the play should be done simply and with no concern for locale or scene, although it may be helpful to have varying levels in the form of blocks, rostra or even tables. These can be the settings for different parts of the action, for elevating the Angel, and particularly for containing the Holy Family, to whom Trowle leads his fellow shepherds. An original tune might be devised for the Angel's words, but otherwise one of the chants in *Plainsong for Schools* (Desclée & Co., Rushworth & Dreaper Ltd.) might serve. Any carol will do for the shepherds' procession.

Mime and gesture are important as the actors themselves will need to convey much that in the theatre is simulated by lighting and effects, including the presence of the star.

These comments are made on the assumption that the play is to be acted in the classroom as a means of teaching it. If more elaborate presentation is contemplated or further information about the text is required, teachers are referred to the present writer's *Seven Miracle Plays* (Oxford) which contains the full adaptation with an introduction and production notes.

# Hand and Eye

This verse is suitable for teaching through visual exercises in a wide variety of media. The notes also contain suggestions for an exercise in recorded sound. (See Ch. 3, p. 17 for further comments on the use of visual and audio-visual media in the teaching of verse.)

The use of paint, chalk or crayon in exercises on nearly all these vivid pieces is too obvious to require special mention. With the exception, therefore, of the first five titles, the notes concentrate on other, less usual, approaches. It should not be assumed, however, that work in the more orthodox media is unsuitable or less valuable than that suggested.

p. 42 **Granton**

p. 43 **The Smuggler**

p. 44 **A Ship sails up to Bideford**

p. 45 **'The General Elliott'**

*Granton*, with its dark tones and slashes of colour, and the second stanza of *The Smuggler*, with its less vivid contrasts, may suggest the making of pictures, particularly perhaps in chalks, on the same or kindred subjects. Work stemming from the other pieces, though, might be inspirational rather than illustrative. Although it is in the starlight that we see the ship sailing into her Devon port, 'the sun is in her hold', and the exotic cargo is an exciting subject for painting.

'*The General Elliott*' might promote the designing and painting of further novel inn signs which have a story behind them.

(*Granton* may also be used as a model for free verse composition—see p. 62.)

p. 46 **The Painting**

The painting in question would appear to be on a Chinese bowl, for the description of two scenes and the inversion of the first stanza to form the last suggest that the writer has turned the bowl round. It would not be an inaccurate reflection of the verse if the class painted a story in the manner of a strip cartoon or, better still, painted two or more scenes forming a decorative sequence when the paper is bent round end to end.

Many pieces to be found in other sections of Book II are, of course, suitable for use with colour media. Among them, the following may be the most useful: *The Ballad of Semmerwater* (p. 19), *The Whale* (p. 23), *The Lonely Scarecrow* (p. 86), *The Ose* (p. 96), *The Doze* (p. 98), *The Marrog* (p. 99), *Gale Warning* (p. 101), *Please to Remember* (p. 104), *In Spring-Time* (p. 125).

p. 47 **Song**

Foliage can be the material for collage work on the same subject. Although there is more scope for this in the country, urban areas in autumn have their supply.

p. 47 **Old Dan'l**

The verse makes an ideal starting point for the collecting of portrait photographs which reveal character, or information about the subject. Newspapers and magazines are obvious sources, but the possibility of the children providing their own photographs is not unrealistic. (See Ch. 3, p. 18 *Children as Photo-*

*graphers.*) Colour transparencies are preferable, not only because they are comparatively easy to take, but also because they can be projected for the whole class to see easily. The good photographer will tell much in a single shot, and this, the children may find, is what the poet does; in *Old Dan'l* words could hardly be used more economically.

p. 48 **The Arrival**  
p. 49 **On These November Evenings**  
p. 51 **November Morning**

These pieces may be used in the same way as recommended for *Old Dan'l* in the preceding note, though here, of course, the photographs need to contain action and convey atmosphere. It is not necessary to confine the class to subjects dealt with by the authors. It will be noted that the feeling of stillness and dampness in the second and third stanzas of *November Morning* is in part the result of 'close-up' images, and without drawing the children's attention to this, an exercise based upon the piece might well use close-ups, or even a sequence of them, as Olive Dehn herself does. An additional exercise on *The Arrival* is the collecting of evocative seaside items.

If other verse with an autumnal flavour is needed, reference may be made to *Please to Remember* (Book II, p. 104), *Fireworks* (Book I, p. 70) or *Autumn Fires* (Book I, p. 70).

p. 52 **A Sheep Fair**

See the two preceding notes.

In addition to finding pictures revealing, say, extremes of climate, the class might suggest sentences, phrases or single words which aptly describe them.

p. 54 **Catalogue**  
p. 55 **August Weather**

As *Catalogue* is a kind of word-montage, the making of a more orthodox photo-montage on the same subject is perhaps an appropriate exercise. (See Ch. 3, p. 17.) Reference might also be made to *Cat* on p. 76 of Book I, and the note about it on p. oo of this book. Further examples of feline behaviour are given in *Marjorie Sitting on the Doorstep* (Book II, p. 105) and *The Cat* (Book II, p. 106). An alternative subject, such as 'Dogs', would also focus attention on the writer's perceptiveness. In a montage on *August Weather*, the emphasis might be on images that capture the colours and feeling of the month, for this, in effect, is what the author herself does. If the exercise is popular, similar work on another month might be undertaken.

p. 56 **Thrushes**  
p. 56 **London to Paris by Air**  
p. 58 **Water Picture**

Language or form make these suitable only for the older children. It is suggested that they try an exercise on seeing things from unusual points of view or in reflection, either by making their own pictures (which they are almost certain to find difficult) or collecting photographs.

As alternatives, *Thrushes* might be approached in a similar way to *Old Dan'l* (see note on p. 52) with which it has something in common; for *London to Paris by Air* and *Water Picture* the making of miniature scenes (with either scrap materials or model toys) is valuable, particularly if, in this instance, the children try to make three-dimensional illustrations of selected passages. A model on *Water Picture* will need a base of mirror glass or, better still, a sheet of polished metal which gives a distorted reflection.

(*Thrushes* may also be used as a model for free verse composition. See p. 63)

p. 59 **The Shining Streets of London** ⎫
p. 60 **Tugs** ⎬

Practically the whole of *The Shining Streets of London* could be the subject of a model. (See previous note.)

Ideally, parts of the model need to be on mirror or polished metal with illumination, both general and, for example, from within (cardboard) buildings. Such an undertaking would probably need a group of children to work on it. Less elaborate exercises more suited to the individual child include painting, illustrations in collage (where again shiny metal is useful) and the collecting of photographs featuring reflections of light, etc.

A similar illustrative model on a reflecting surface is suggested for *Tugs*. Toy boats are not likely to appear as authentic as those the children make themselves out of wood, plasticine or modelling clay. The use of light is, of course, a necessary refinement, if there is to be the same kind of contrast shown as that which the writer describes. Steel (no. 17) cinemoid is the best colour medium for giving an overall night effect. (See note on p. 37 about *The Moon* and *Moon Magic*.) With ingenuity and skill common enough in the junior school, coloured battery-operated navigation lights can be rigged on the tugs. The alternative of using tin foil to represent the lanterns will only be effective in white light or daylight.

p. 60 **The Magnifying Glass** ⎫
p. 61 **The Flight of Birds** ⎬

On p. 18 of Ch. 3 directions are given for the making of glass slides for use with a projector. It is suggested that both *The Magnifying Glass* and *The Flight of Birds* offer excellent opportunities for the children to make and use their own slides, and that these are better here than transparencies which, however appropriate, are unlikely to be more than illustrative.

For *The Magnifying Glass* slides made with pieces of foliage and scrap materials (preferably translucent) are recommended. They assume quite different features when magnified in projection, and the children will doubtless comment on the images and suggest identities, just as the poet does. The poem (its title refers, surely, to the glass that magnifies rather than the instrument itself) is a valuable piece for showing what can be seen when viewed with a poet's eye in processes normally thought of as scientific. This approach is tidier and more exciting than an alternative exercise in magnification in which the class have to be equipped with lenses. Another way of teaching *The Magnifying Glass* is through the making of fantasy pictures (in any suitable medium) from a study of common objects and substances.

For *A Flight of Birds*, a sequence of abstract slides which reflects both the flight and *the sounds* can accompany a reading. Making the slides and choosing the sequence is not the easiest of creative activities, but it promotes desirable concentration on the poem and the results can be highly original. In addition to scrap materials, paint smears may be useful in this instance. The speaking of the poem is best done solo, in a series of solos, or in groups. Two words which are likely to need explaining are:

> *starnels* (line 3)—starlings
> *suthers* (line 7)—makes a rushing noise.

For further slide work, *The Banjo Player* (Book II, p. 29) is recommended. It can be the core of a miniature performance in which abstract projections reflect the moods and images of the verse as a solo voice speaks the lines. With practice, even the cuts, mixes and superimposes of film and television can be introduced, and there is the possibility of using a recording of a banjo from the second stanza on. When projection equipment is not available, *The Banjo Player* can be the subject of contrasting paintings or drawings. Used in this way, the exercise becomes the visual counterpart of the dramatic work described on p. 49 of this book.

*Owl* (Book II, p. 120) might be used in a similar sort of exercise, using different voices, abstract slides, and perhaps a recording of an owl (e.g. HMV CLP 1723. *A Tapestry of British Birdsong*).

p. 61 **Village Sounds**

An audial exercise using a tape recorder is suggested. It is best not to produce the sounds described but to find those of another, perhaps contrasting, situation, such as the street on a winter's morning. Many sounds can be simulated orally in the classroom or playground, but for the latter a battery tape recorder is necessary and if this is available there is novelty in actually going 'on location' for them. The best final results are obtained through editing, (see Ch. 3, p. 19). A reading of the verse might be the starting point for the exercise. If it is used again after the children have worked on a tape, they may be struck by the poet's ability to listen.

Alternative ways of teaching *Village Sounds* through literary exercises are noted on p. 56 and p. 61.

(Although there are only a few sound images in *The Cat* (Book II, p. 106), the poem conveys strongly the feeling of a summer night and can suggest the sort of sound which might be used in a recorded 'sound poem' on night.)

# Imagine That!

The verse in this section may be taught through creative work using language —in most instances, stories or other prose compositions. (See Ch. 3, p. 19 for further comments.)

p. 64 **Smells**
p. 65 **Names for Twins**
p. 67 **What is Grey?**
p. 68 **What is White?**

The writers have provided lists, which the children may appreciate more when they have made up some of their own on the same or different subjects. It is suggested that there should be no attempt at rhyming, which would be restricting. *Smells* might suggest brief statements, similar to Christopher Morley's, on other senses. Naming need not be confined to twins but include, for example, partners (eg. Merry & Bright—comedians). It is a practice hallowed by English literature and having humbler affinities with the card game of *Happy Families*. *What is Grey?* and *What is White?* obviously invite similar thoughts about other colours, but for the exercise to be of maximum value, the originality of the writer's choice needs to be noted and emulated whenever possible. It will also be seen that she sometimes uses the colours to describe feelings, etc., as well as things, and this is worth attempting. The exercise makes excellent oral work, but the most original lists are usually produced in writing. The former approach is particularly useful perhaps as an introduction.

*Song* (Book II, p. 47) and *Village Sounds* (Book II, p. 61) are additional material. For easier pieces see *Shining Things* (Book I, p. 84), *Noise* (Book I, p. 86), *Boys' and Girls' Names* (Book I, p. 87) and *Slowly* (Book I, p. 44).

(The list has value in the writing of free verse. See notes on pp. 23 and 63.)

p. 69 **Digging**

A contemplative poem, very different from the straightforward catalogue called *Smells* (Book II, p. 64), with which it has some affinity. Though not even the older children may be expected to understand its full significance, it is written in simple language and is suitable for children to use in a list exercise (see preceding note) in which they name scents of their own choice. But they, like the poet, should perhaps try to say what each scent means to them. A similar exercise can be done on sounds.

p. 70 **Fairy Things**
p. 71 **The Wood-Cutter's Night Song**

See first note in this section. Clare writes vividly but not exhaustively, and the children could make a list of other things which might be used by fairies or small people such as Lilliputians. They should say, of course, what each was used for.

Teachers might find working on *Fairy Things* an apt opportunity for introducing Shakespeare by quoting from *Romeo and Juliet* what Mercutio says about Queen Mab:

> . . . . . she comes
> In shape no bigger than an agate-stone
> On the fore-finger of an alderman,
> Drawn with a team of little atomies
> Athwart men's noses as they lie asleep:
> Her waggon-spokes made of long spinners' legs;
> The cover, of the wings of grasshoppers;
> The traces, of the smallest spider's web;
> The collars, of the moonshine's watery beams;
> Her whip of cricket's bone; the lash, of film;
> Her waggoner, a small grey-coated gnat. . . . . .
> Her chariot is an empty hazel-nut,
> Made by the joiner squirrel or old grub,
> Time out o' mind the fairies' coachmakers.
> And in this state, she gallops night by night. . . . . .

Before work begins on *The Wood-Cutter's Night Song*, it will probably be advisable to elaborate a little on the archaic situation described, and perhaps explain such expressions as 'Bill and mittens, lie ye there!' and 'Supper hanging on the hooks'. After a reading of the poem, the children could list information about the wood-cutter which the poem hints at but does not state overtly, such as what sort of man he is, features of his life, etc. Their appreciation of the poet's observation and expression may be encouraged if they list the thoughts of a present-day man or woman who is setting out for home after a day at the factory, office, shop, etc. This could also be the subject of a composition written in the first person.

p. 72 **November**
p. 73 **Hay Harvest**
p. 74 **Down with the Holly, Ivy, All . . .**

It may be thought logical to move from the list-making exercises recommended in the previous notes to the writing of compositions conveying atmosphere and personal feeling, especially of course by means of original turns of phrase. Always, it is urged, should composition of this kind reflect the writer's true feelings as he remembers them; false sentiments make unconvincing prose. *November* might inspire writing about another month; *Hay Harvest*, some experience of early morning or, conversely, late evening. The emotional content of *Down with the Holly, Ivy, All . . .* may be harder to find, but with its three opening lines each beginning 'Down with . . .' and the final words 'And let all sport with Christmas die', there is, surely, a strong impression that the fun (or 'sport' as Herrick has it) is over, and life must go back to normal. This end-of-Christmas feeling is what might be recounted, or perhaps it might be contrasted with the anticipation of the pre-Christmas period. If so, use might also be made of *In the Week when Christmas Comes* (Book I, p. 18).

The customs and superstitions mentioned by Herrick will doubtless need explaining. The notion is still held that devils will spring from every leaf of holly left up after Twelfth Night (in Herrick's day, it was Candlemas, the 2nd of February), but it is unlikely that the children will know of the custom of laying up the remains of the yule log 'to tend the Christmas log next year'. Of significance, too, is the reference to the white loaf—that is, best bread. The pie would have been of minced meat and dried plums—the sort of pie Little Jack Horner had.

p. 74 **Peter to Tea**
p. 76 **The New Boy**
p. 77 **Anne and the Field-Mouse**
p. 78 **The Rescue**
p. 80 **At the Theatre**

It is revealing for the children to compare the verse with their own narrative compositions on the same or similar subjects. The more interesting approach is to have the composition work done first and to look at the verse afterwards. The pieces are particularly valuable, either because they tell of experiences which the children themselves have had or because they are about incidents in which they could easily have been involved. Even *At the Theatre* can be related to a situation which appears to be common enough when the family is watching television. The children should be advised to draw on their actual experiences whenever possible, for this usually results in lively writing.

p. 81 **The Apple Tree**
p. 83 **The Fugitive**

Kindred pieces which, instead of telling a whole story, take a part out of one, and leave the reader to speculate on the rest. The class might give their own full versions in the form of tales of adventure. Who was it who was hiding in the apple tree? Was he scouting for real Indians? Why was the man running and why did he have a knife? Why did he run off again? Who is the subject of *The Fugitive* and why is he being pursued? Who are the men looking for him and why, after they have passed, do they suddenly draw rein and one of them say 'Hush!' What happens next? These are some of the questions in the narratives which need to be answered. In both, the accounts might be written from the point of view of pursuer or pursued. The value of the exercise is seen when the children realise how, in a few lines, the poets have stimulated so much thought.

### p. 84 My Bonny Lad

See previous note, but here in this Northumbrian folk-song there is a less sensational situation. A woman asks another person, presumably a man, whether there is any news of her 'bonny lad'. Is he well? He had gone away to 'moor the keel', i.e. to work with one of the flat-bottomed Tyne boats. She is told that he has been seen at sea, but that he is now drowned. The class might devise the story behind the conversation.

Another piece upon which to base a dramatic story is *The Gipsy Laddie* (Book II, p. 17). In particular the lady's feelings and her life as a gipsy might be worth considering in view of the hint of regret in the final stanza.

### p. 84 The Ship
### p. 85 At the Railway Station, Upway
### p. 85 The Twa Corbies

See note on *The Apple Tree* and *The Fugitive*. Again, each poem tells only part of a story, and the recommended exercise is for the class to write fuller versions. But here the situations might be seen in a present-day context and the accounts written as news items, suitably headed and sub-headed perhaps. The material has striking, even sensational, qualities: a ship, empty and battered and with a tired but proud crew, returns home unwelcomed after a long voyage; waiting for a train, a child plays a fiddle and a convict grimly sings a song about freedom (why was he there? Had he escaped and been recaptured?); a man lies killed, his body the prey of birds, but his wife has 'ta'en anither mate' (did either or both of them murder him?).

The form of *The Twa Corbies* will need explaining to some classes, but they may be able to work out the ballad for themselves if they are told that it is a conversation between two crows. It may also help if certain words are translated for them, in particular:

*mane* (stanza 1): moan

*fail dyke* (stanza 2): a wall built of turves

*hause-bane* (stanza 4): breast bone

*theek* (stanza 4): thatch

p. 86 **The Snail**

p. 86 **The Lonely Scarecrow**

p. 87 **On a Cat, Ageing**

> To see things from an unusual standpoint is an attribute of the poet and the artist, and the snail's attitude may therefore seem reasonable if we accept the anthropomorphic qualities John Gay gives him. It stirs children's imagination and helps them appreciate this side of the poet's work if they write about things seen through eyes other than their own. They might describe a garden as a bird might see it—and here, of course, the snail will be viewed in a way which has escaped his notice in Gay's verse. Complementary to *The Lonely Scarecrow* might be a composition about the thoughts of a guy on a bonfire. To use *On a Cat, Ageing* in a similar way will require more imaginative effort, as children have little concept of old age. If, however, they make a point of watching an old cat carefully, they should manage it.

p. 87 **The Fly**

p. 88 **Under Ground**

p. 89 **The Dumb Soldier**

> Obviously *The Fly* has similarities with *Fairy Things* by John Clare (Book II, p. 70, and note on p. 57 of this book), but whereas Clare is always looking downwards with human eyes, de la Mare, on the other hand, imagines he is seeing things as a fly sees them. It is suggested that the class should write from the point of view of a small creature. They might also imagine the *feelings* of one of the animals or insects mentioned by James Reeves in *Under Ground*, particularly when they explore or, as he reminds us, when the human world intrudes. The toy soldier of Stevenson's poem is not, it will be seen, actually buried, but hidden in an open hole. This gives him a different point of view which the class might consider and write about—an appropriate exercise in the light of the poet's comments in the last stanza.

> (Other verse, such as *Song of the Year* (Book I, p. 78) or *Thrushes* (Book II, p. 56), can be used as additional material for exercises of the kind suggested above.)

# Models

The pieces in this section are chosen to provide children with models for their own verse composition. In most instances, it is the form of the verse that will encourage them, but some pieces may do so by virtue of subject matter. The verse forms are the limerick, the clerihew, simple ballad rhyming *a, b, c, b,* and free verse. Other short verse forms, such as the haiku, have not been included because they are more difficult than they appear to be, and are better suited to secondary school teaching. (See also Ch. 3, p. 21. Original Verse.)

p. 92 **There was an Old Man with a Beard**
p. 92 **There was an Old Man in a Barge**
p. 92 **There was an Old Man of Peru**
p. 93 **Obvious Reasons**
p. 93 **There was a Young Lady of Sheen**
p. 93 **A Cheerful Old Bear at the Zoo**
p. 94 **Kindness to Animals**

A range of limericks, beginning with two of Edward Lear's which have the same rhyme words for their first and last lines. The models then become more difficult as three rhyme words and verbal surprises are introduced, but there is no example of the most advanced sort of limerick where, in addition to linguistic twists, there is also an epigrammatic quality. The children are not likely to produce any but simple pieces themselves; the purpose of the selection, however, is that rather than work from one title at a time, they should see several versions and gain a general impression of form. It may be questioned whether *Kindness to Animals* is a true limerick, but its inclusion for the present purpose would seem wholly justified. Its first lines may be doubtful, but they are excellent prototypes.

p. 95 **Dr. W. G. Grace**

The clerihew provides an alternative to the limerick (see preceding note). It is a four-lined verse rhyming *a, a, b, b,* and is about a person whose name appears in the first line. Sometimes the name is the whole of the first line, as here. The lines need not scan and they may be of any length. In content clerihews are usually absurd or facetious.

p. 95 **My Aunt**

It is suggested that the class write down the first two lines and then go on to make their own list of items, using the same rhyme scheme and line pattern. Alternate four feet and three feet lines, rhyming *a, b, c, b,* are a fairly easy metrical form to handle.

For more serious verse writing and using four line stanzas with only one rhyme, *Village Sounds* (Book II, p. 61) is a useful model. Of some dozen other pieces in WAYS employing the same kind of ballad form and meter, the following may be the most acceptable as additional material: *Wheelbarrow* (Book I, p. 36), *The Three Singing Birds* (Book I, p. 65), *The Princess and the Gipsies* Book II, p. 27).

p. 96 **The Osc**

p. 98 **The Doze**

p. 99 **The Marrog**

> When working on the limerick, etc., it is the form of the verse that suggests the content; here the models may be used for the ideas they give, and the children encouraged to write about their own original beasts and space monsters. When subjects are fantastic and/or humorous, such matters as verse form usually take care of themselves, but it is of little importance if the children's work is technically weak, provided it is interesting and imaginative. With these models it usually is. (See also Ch. 3, p. 22.)

> *The Hippocrump* (Book I, p. 82) is additional material.

p. 100 **The Horny-Goloch**

> See preceding note; but a horny-goloch (Scottish) is a real creature—a stag beetle. The children might be asked to devise an original and descriptive name for some other insect and to write about it in a few lines of verse.

> *hantle*: a great many

p. 100 **Fog**

p. 100 **Wind and Silver**

p. 101 **The Runner**

> It is suggested that, as an introduction to the writing of free verse, the class should have these three pieces read aloud to them; to hear free verse spoken is the best way of feeling its rhythm and gaining an idea of why it is verse and not prose. (See Ch. 3, p. 23 for a further note.) The children can try their hands on practically any subject, but it is best if early efforts stem from given titles, are brief, and are confined to a single thought or image. Weather, colours, the elements, the seasons, animals and birds are general areas from which titles might be taken.

p. 101 **Roses**

p. 101 **Gale Warning**

p. 102 **Bats**

> These are best used after introductory work of the sort suggested in the preceding note. They may help widen the scope of the children's own writing. (Some children may notice that there are a few rhymes in *Bats* and ask whether it is free verse, therefore. If this question comes up—but only, it is suggested, *if* it does—it can be pointed out that some free verse writers do slip in a rhyme here and there, either co-incidentally or because they feel it helps the rhythm, but that the lines of *Bats* have an irregular rhythm and this is what makes us term it free verse.)

> Other pieces which may be used as models are *Granton* (Book II, p. 42) and

*Thrushes* (Book II, p. 56). If the class have done the kind of 'list' exercises described in the notes on IMAGINE THAT! (pp. 56 and 57), some of their material may be adaptable to free verse form. (See note in Ch. 3, p. 23.)

# Listen Again!

As in Book I, the final section is of verse to be read aloud. Although it is anticipated that teachers will choose what they need from the section, the verse is arranged to provide variety of treatment and form, if read in sequence. (For comments, see Ch. 3, p. 24.)

p. 104 **Please to Remember**

p. 105 **Marjorie Sitting on the Doorstep**
p. 106 **The Cat**
p. 107 **Out at Night**

Each could be used as starting points for composition on the cats' thoughts, written perhaps from the cats' points of view. The exercise can encourage imaginative thought, but does not help directly in the study of the verse. For this reason it has not been included in IMAGINE THAT! Some 'joining in' may, of course, be expected in a reading of *Out at Night*.

p. 108 **The Quangle Wangle's Hat**

Although the piece can be spoken chorally with individual parts and groups of speakers, it was thought inadvisable to include it in MANY VOICES, because of its length and the difficulty of saying together some of the lines.

p. 110 **The Policeman**

See also *The Policeman* (Book I, p. 101).

p. 111 **I've Got an Apple Ready**

A particularly useful expression of an experience which most children have had, but few will admit to.

p. 112 **Wonders of Modern Science**

Some teachers may care to explain *parody*, and use this piece as an example.

p. 112 **Conkers**

p. 114 **Sweet Chestnuts**

p. 115 **A Visit from the Sea**

p. 116 **A Spike of Green**

p. 116 **The Helicopter**

p. 117 **The Bat** See also *Bats* (Book II, p. 102).

p. 117 **Moonlit Apples**

p. 118 **Priest's Hole**

>Not all the children are likely to know what a priest's hole is, and before reading the piece, it will be necessary to explain that, in the 17th century, Roman Catholic priests were persecuted and many houses had special hiding places for them concealed behind secret panels, etc.

p. 119 **The Snake**

p. 120 **Owl**   See note on p. 55 about use of the verse in practical work.

p. 120 **Cuckoos**

p. 121 **The Hens**

p. 123 **Martha of Bethany**

>The poem is concerned with the incident related in St. Luke, Ch. 10, vv. 38–end. It comes from *The Witnesses*, a collection of poems by Clive Sansom. Each poem is written from the point of view of a person who knew or saw Christ on earth. Many, like this one, are in the form of a dramatic speech.
>
>The class may express surprise at this approach to a biblical character and a biblical situation. If so, it might be pointed out that what Clive Sansom does is to put himself, in imagination, into the setting of a recorded event, in rather the same way that we may do in thinking about verse like *The Gipsy Laddie* (Book II, p. 17 and see note on p. 47 of this book).

p. 124 **The Fog**

>A particularly striking poem if it is read to the children for the first time when their books are closed.

p. 125 **In Spring-Time**

p. 126 **Target Area**

It is suggested that the four following poems (and perhaps *The Oxen* also) should be reserved for the oldest children. There is nothing unsuitable for younger children in them, but each is of a contemplative kind. They are thought of as bridges to poetry in secondary education.

p. 127 **Cock-Crow**

p. 128 **Something Told the Wild Geese**

p. 129 **The Runaway**

p. 129 **The Ballad of Billy Rose**

>*Fishponds:* a district of Bristol.

p. 132 **The Oxen**

>*barton:* cowshed   *coombe:* valley

# Index of Titles

|  |  | Book | Page |
|---|---|---|---|
| Aeroplane | *Mary McB. Green* | I | 7 |
| After a Bath | *Aileen Fisher* | I | 57 |
| Aiken Drum |  | I | 42 |
| Anne and the Field-Mouse | *Ian Serraillier* | II | 77 |
| Apple Song | *Clive Sansom* | I | 30 |
| Apple Tree, The | *James Stephens* | II | 81 |
| Arrival, The | *John Walsh* | II | 48 |
| At the Railway Station, Upway | *Thomas Hardy* | II | 85 |
| At the Theatre | *A. P. Herbert* | II | 80 |
| August Weather | *Katherine Tynan* | II | 55 |
| Autumn Fires | *Robert Louis Stevenson* | I | 70 |
|  |  |  |  |
| Ballad of Billy Rose, The | *Leslie Norris* | II | 129 |
| Ballad of Semmerwater, The | *William Watson* | II | 19 |
| Band, The |  | I | 38 |
| Banjo Player, The | *Clifford Dyment* | II | 29 |
| Bat, The | *Theodore Roethke* | II | 117 |
| Bats | *Randall Jarrell* | II | 102 |
| Bats | *Winifred Kingdon-Ward* | I | 17 |
| Berries | *Walter de la Mare* | I | 93 |
| Block City | *Robert Louis Stevenson* | I | 102 |
| Bold Piglet, The | *'Old Shepherd'* | I | 108 |
| Boys' and Girls' Names | *Eleanor Farjeon* | I | 87 |
|  |  |  |  |
| Cat | *Mary B. Miller* | I | 76 |
| Cat, The | *Richard Church* | II | 106 |
| Cat came Fiddling, A |  | I | 4 |
| Catalogue | *Rosalie Moore* | II | 54 |
| Ceremonial Band, The | *James Reeves* | II | 10 |
| Cheerful old Bear at the Zoo, A |  | II | 93 |

|  |  | Book | Page |
|---|---|---|---|
| Choosing Shoes | ffrida Wolfe | I | 34 |
| Christmas Everywhere | Phillips Brooks | II | 15 |
| Christmas Morning | Elizabeth Madox Roberts | I | 116 |
| Clown, The | Dorothy Aldis | I | 74 |
| Clucking Hen, The |  | I | 15 |
| Cock-Crow | Edward Thomas | II | 127 |
| Conjuror | Clive Sansom | I | 21 |
| Conkers | Clive Sansom | II | 112 |
| Cowboy Spring |  | I | 23 |
| Cuckoos | Andrew Young | II | 120 |
| | | | |
| Dabbling in the Dew |  | I | 31 |
| Dachshund | Clive Sansom | I | 104 |
| Daddy Fell into the Pond | Alfred Noyes | I | 95 |
| Dance, Thumbkin, Dance |  | I | 48 |
| Dancing Cabman, The | J. B. Morton | II | 14 |
| December |  | I | 4 |
| Digging | Edward Thomas | II | 69 |
| Down with the Holly, Ivy, All . . . | Robert Herrick | II | 74 |
| Doze, The | James Reeves | II | 98 |
| Dr. W. G. Grace | E. C. Bentley | II | 95 |
| Ducks' Ditty | Kenneth Grahame | I | 37 |
| Dumb Soldier, The | Robert Louis Stevenson | II | 89 |
| Dustman, The | Clive Sansom | I | 8 |
| | | | |
| Engine Driver, The | Clive Sansom | I | 28 |
| Engineers | Jimmy Garthwaite | I | 6 |
| Every Time I Climb a Tree | David McCord | I | 96 |
| | | | |
| Fairies of the Caldon Low, The | Mary Howitt | I | 109 |
| Fairy Things | John Clare | II | 70 |
| Fifteen Acres, The | James Stephens | II | 2 |
| Fireworks | James Reeves | I | 70 |
| Flight of Birds, The | John Clare | II | 61 |
| Fly, The | Walter de la Mare | II | 87 |
| Fog | Carl Sandburg | II | 100 |
| Fog, The | W. H. Davies | II | 124 |
| French and English | Thomas Hood | I | 63 |
| Fugitive, The | Dorothy Margaret Stuart | II | 83 |

| | | Book | Page |
|---|---|---|---|
| Gale Warning | Michael Roberts | II | 101 |
| Garden Year, The | Sara Coleridge | I | 77 |
| 'General Elliott, The' | Robert Graves | II | 45 |
| Gipsy Laddie, The | | II | 17 |
| Granton | Norman MacCaig | II | 42 |
| | | | |
| Hay Harvest | Patrick R. Chalmers | II | 73 |
| Helicopter, The | Ian Serraillier | II | 116 |
| Hens, The | Elizabeth Madox Roberts | II | 121 |
| Here we Come A-Piping | | I | 2 |
| Here we Come Gathering! | Noel Holmes | I | 32 |
| Here we go Round the Mulberry Bush | | I | 49 |
| Hippocrump, The | James Reeves | I | 82 |
| Ho, Dandelion! | Mary Mapes Dodge | I | 26 |
| Horny-Goloch, The | | II | 100 |
| Hunting Song | | II | 24 |
| | | | |
| In Spring-Time | W. H. Davies | II | 125 |
| In the Week when Christmas Comes | Eleanor Farjeon | I | 18 |
| Indian Summer on the Prairie, An | Vachel Lindsay | II | 13 |
| I've got an Apple Ready | John Walsh | II | 111 |
| | | | |
| Jumblies, The | Edward Lear | II | 6 |
| | | | |
| Kindness to Animals | Laura Richards | II | 94 |
| King of China's Daughter, The | Edith Sitwell | I | 90 |
| Kings came Riding | Charles Williams | I | 81 |
| King's High Drummer, The | Caryl Brahms | I | 27 |
| Knight Whose Armour Didn't Squeak, The | A. A. Milne | I | 105 |
| | | | |
| Lachlan Gorach's Rhyme | | I | 52 |
| Land of Counterpane, The | Robert Louis Stevenson | I | 88 |
| Leave her, Johnny | | II | 22 |
| Little Trotty Wagtail | John Clare | I | 75 |
| London to Paris by Air | Lord Ronald Gorell | II | 56 |
| Lonely Scarecrow, The | James Kirkup | II | 86 |
| | | | |
| Magnifying Glass, The | Walter de la Mare | II | 60 |
| Main-Deep, The | James Stephens | II | 5 |
| Man in the Moon stayed up Too Late, The | J. R. R. Tolkien | I | 113 |

|  |  | Book | Page |
|---|---|---|---|
| Marching Song | *Thomas Hardy* | II | 5 |
| Marjorie Sitting on the Doorstep | *John Walsh* | II | 105 |
| Marrog, The | *R. C. Scriven* | II | 99 |
| Martha of Bethany | *Clive Sansom* | II | 123 |
| Month of Liverpool, The |  | I | 100 |
| Moon Magic | *Pamela Tennant* | I | 80 |
| Moon, The | *Robert Louis Stevenson* | I | 78 |
| Moonlit Apples | *John Drinkwater* | II | 117 |
| Mr. Tom Narrow | *James Reeves* | I | 103 |
| Mrs. Peck-Pigeon | *Eleanor Farjeon* | I | 56 |
| Mrs. Utter | *James Reeves* | I | 92 |
| Mud | *Polly C. Boyden* | I | 55 |
| My Aunt |  | II | 95 |
| My Bonny Lad |  | II | 84 |
| Mysterious Cat, The | *Vachel Lindsay* | I | 46 |
| Names for Twins | *Alastair Reed* | II | 65 |
| New Boy, The | *John Walsh* | II | 76 |
| Noah | *James Reeves* | I | 71 |
| Noise | *J. Pope* | I | 86 |
| November | *John Clare* | II | 72 |
| November Morning | *Olive Dehn* | II | 51 |
| Oats and Beans and Barley |  | I | 50 |
| Obvious Reasons | *Lewis Carroll* | II | 93 |
| Old Dan'l | *L. A. G. Strong* | II | 47 |
| Old King Cole |  | I | 40 |
| Old Zip Coon | *David Stevens* | II | 12 |
| Oliver Cromwell |  | II | 21 |
| On a Cat, Ageing | *Alexander Gray* | II | 87 |
| On these November Evenings | *John Walsh* | II | 49 |
| Open Windows | *Alexander Franklin* | I | 68 |
| Oranges and Lemons |  | I | 33 |
| Osc, The | *James Reeves* | II | 96 |
| Out at Night | *John Walsh* | II | 107 |
| Outside | *Eleanor Farjeon* | I | 104 |
| Owl | *Randall Jarrell* | II | 120 |
| Owl and the Pussy-Cat, The | *Edward Lear* | I | 14 |
| Oxen, The | *Thomas Hardy* | II | 132 |

|  |  | Book | Page |
|---|---|---|---|
| Painting, The | Oscar Wilde | II | 42 |
| Pancake, The | Christina Rossetti | I | 4 |
| Peter to Tea | John Walsh | II | 74 |
| Piper, A | Seumas O'Sullivan | II | 2 |
| Piper O' Dundee, The |  | II | 20 |
| Please to Remember | Walter de la Mare | II | 104 |
| Policeman, The | Clive Sansom | I | 101 |
| Policeman, The | Jan Struther | II | 110 |
| Postman, The | Clive Sansom | I | 8 |
| Priest's Hole | Gregory Harrison | II | 118 |
| Princess and the Gipsies, The | Frances Cornford | II | 27 |
|  |  |  |  |
| Quack! | Walter de la Mare | I | 12 |
| Quangle Wangle's Hat, The | Edward Lear | II | 108 |
| Queen Nefertiti |  | I | 35 |
|  |  |  |  |
| Rescue, The | Hal Summers | II | 78 |
| Robert of Lincoln | William Cullen Bryant | I | 19 |
| Roses | George Eliot | II | 101 |
| Roundabout, The | Clive Sansom | I | 3 |
| Run a Little | James Reeves | I | 53 |
| Runaway, The | Robert Frost | II | 129 |
| Runner, The | Walt Whitman | II | 101 |
|  |  |  |  |
| Sage's Pigtail, The | W. M. Thackeray | I | 61 |
| Sampan |  | I | 9 |
| Scarecrow | Eleanor Farjeon | I | 2 |
| Sea Gull, The | Elizabeth Coatsworth | I | 9 |
| Sheep Fair, A | Thomas Hardy | II | 52 |
| Shepherds, The | Alexander Franklin (adapter) | II | 32 |
| Shining Streets of London, The | Alfred Noyes | II | 59 |
| Shining Things | Elizabeth Gould | I | 84 |
| Ship, The | J. C. Squire | II | 84 |
| Ship sails up to Bideford, A | Herbert Asquith | II | 44 |
| Sing a Song of Honey | Barbara Euphan Todd | I | 24 |
| Sink Song | J. A. Lindon | I | 5 |
| Skipping Song | John Walsh | I | 59 |
| Slowly | James Reeves | I | 44 |
| Smells | Christopher Morley | II | 64 |
| Smuggler, The |  | II | 43 |

|  |  | Book | Page |
|---|---|---|---|
| Snail, The | John Gay | II | 86 |
| Snake, The | Emily Dickinson | II | 119 |
| Soldier, Soldier |  | I | 64 |
| Something Told the Wild Geese | Rachel Field | II | 128 |
| Song | Richard Watson Dixon | II | 47 |
| Song for a Ball-Game | Wilfrid Thorley | I | 58 |
| Song of the Year, The | Irene Gough | I | 78 |
| Spike of Green, A | Barbara Baker | II | 116 |
| Steeple, The | Elizabeth Fleming | II | 25 |
| Stocking and Shirt | James Reeves | I | 98 |
| Sweet Chestnuts | John Walsh | II | 114 |
|  |  |  |  |
| Tailor | Eleanor Farjeon | I | 13 |
| Target Area | Peter Roberts | II | 126 |
| There are Big Waves | Eleanor Farjeon | I | 56 |
| There was an Old Man in a Barge | Edward Lear | II | 92 |
| There was an Old Man of Peru |  | II | 92 |
| There was an Old Man with a Beard | Edward Lear | II | 92 |
| There was a Young Lady of Sheen |  | II | 93 |
| Three Singing Birds, The | James Reeves | I | 65 |
| Thrushes | Humbert Wolfe | II | 56 |
| Tide Rises, The Tide Falls, The | Henry Wadsworth Longfellow | II | 15 |
| Tiger-Lilies | Thomas Bailey Aldrich | II | 16 |
| Toy Band, The | Henry Newbolt | II | 9 |
| Tugs | George Rostrevor Hamilton | II | 60 |
| Twa Corbies, The |  | II | 85 |
|  |  |  |  |
| Uncle John's Pig | ffrida Wolfe | I | 115 |
| Under Ground | James Reeves | II | 88 |
| Under the Tent of the Sky | Rowena Bennett | I | 73 |
|  |  |  |  |
| Village Sounds | James Reeves | II | 61 |
| Visit from the Sea, A | Robert Louis Stevenson | II | 115 |
|  |  |  |  |
| Water Picture | May Swenson | II | 58 |
| Whale, The |  | II | 23 |
| What is Grey? | Mary O'Neill | II | 67 |
| What is White? | Mary O'Neill | II | 68 |
| Wheelbarrow | Eleanor Farjeon | I | 36 |
| Where Go the Boats? | Robert Louis Stevenson | I | 91 |

|  |  | Book | Page |
|---|---|---|---|
| White Fields | *James Stephens* | I | 69 |
| Wife of Usher's Well, The |  | II | 30 |
| Wind and Silver | *Amy Lowell* | II | 100 |
| Windy Nights | *Rodney Bennett* | I | 5 |
| Windy Old Weather |  | I | 22 |
| Wonders of Modern Science |  | II | 112 |
| Wood-Cutter's Night Song, The | *John Clare* | II | 71 |
| Wynken, Blynken and Nod | *Eugene Field* | I | 99 |

# Index of First Lines

|                                                    | Book | Page |
|----------------------------------------------------|------|------|
| A bat is born                                      | II   | 102  |
| A cat came fiddling out of a barn                  | I    | 4    |
| A cheerful old bear at the zoo                     | II   | 93   |
| A glimpse of a pram through the window             | II   | 74   |
| A narrow fellow in the grass                       | II   | 119  |
| A piper in the streets today                       | II   | 2    |
| A scandalous man                                   | I    | 103  |
| A shadow is floating through the moonlight         | II   | 120  |
| A ship sails up to Bideford                        | II   | 44   |
| A shunting engine butts them                       | II   | 42   |
| After my bath                                      | I    | 57   |
| All along the backwater                            | I    | 37   |
| Alone on the lawn                                  | II   | 14   |
| Along the rim of sea and sky                       | II   | 116  |
| Along the valley of the Ump                        | I    | 82   |
| 'And where have you been, my Mary . . . . .?'      | I    | 109  |
| As I looked out one May morning                    | II   | 27   |
| As I was walking all alane                         | II   | 85   |
| As we were a-fishing off Haisborough light         | I    | 22   |
| At noon three English dowagers ride                | II   | 60   |
| At the top of the house the apples are laid in rows| II   | 117  |
|                                                    |      |      |
| Bounce ball! Bounce ball!                          | I    | 58   |
| By day the bat is cousin to the mouse              | II   | 117  |
|                                                    |      |      |
| Cats sleep fat and walk thin                       | II   | 54   |
| Christmas Eve, and twelve of the clock             | II   | 132  |
|                                                    |      |      |
| Dance, Thumbkin, dance                             | I    | 48   |
| Dark brown is the river                            | I    | 91   |

|  | Book | Page |
|---|---|---|
| Dead heat and windless air | II | 55 |
| Dear Madam, you have seen this play | II | 80 |
| Deep asleep, deep asleep | II | 19 |
| Down along the orchard | I | 30 |
| Down with the rosemary, and so | II | 74 |
| Dreary lay the long road, dreary lay the town | II | 9 |
| Dr. W. G. Grace | II | 95 |
| | | |
| Each pair of twins | II | 65 |
| Every few hours | II | 110 |
| Every Thursday morning | I | 8 |
| Every time I climb a tree | I | 96 |
| Everyone grumbled. The sky was grey. | I | 95 |
| Everywhere, everywhere, Christmas to-night! | II | 15 |
| | | |
| Far from the loud sea beaches | II | 115 |
| First the heel | I | 52 |
| | | |
| Gay go up, and gay go down | I | 33 |
| Greatly shining | II | 100 |
| Grey is the colour of an elephant | II | 67 |
| Grey lichens, mid thy hills of creeping thyme | II | 70 |
| | | |
| Hark! She is calling to her cat | II | 106 |
| He blinks upon the hearth-rug | II | 87 |
| He dumped her in the wheelbarrow | I | 36 |
| He fell in victory's fierce pursuit | II | 45 |
| He takes an empty hat — | I | 21 |
| He was Bang bang-banging on his | I | 27 |
| Here am I | II | 104 |
| Here we come a-piping | I | 2 |
| Here we go round the mulberry bush | I | 49 |
| He's pulling on his boots! | I | 104 |
| Hev ye seen owt of maa bonny lad | II | 84 |
| Hi, Mr. Scarecrow! | I | 2 |
| Ho, Dandelion! my lightsome fellow! | I | 26 |
| Honey from the white rose, honey from the red | I | 24 |
| How large unto the tiny fly | II | 87 |
| How still the woods were! Not a redbreast whistled | II | 114 |

|  | Book | Page |
|---|---|---|
| I cling and swing | II | 2 |
| I like noise | I | 86 |
| I like not lady-slippers | II | 16 |
| I like to see | I | 74 |
| I love all shining things—the lovely moon | I | 84 |
| I met a man mowing | II | 73 |
| I saw a little tailor sitting stitch, stitch, stitching | I | 13 |
| I saw a proud, mysterious cat | I | 46 |
| I saw the fog grow thick | II | 124 |
| I was hiding in the crooked apple tree | II | 81 |
| If Bethlehem were here today | I | 116 |
| In the deep kingdom under ground | II | 88 |
| In the other gardens | I | 70 |
| In the pond in the park | II | 58 |
| In the winter time we go | I | 69 |
| It was in the year of forty-four | II | 23 |
| It was late last night when the Squire came home | II | 17 |
| It's all very well | II | 123 |
| | | |
| January brings burning heat, and red dust dims the sun | I | 78 |
| January brings the snow | I | 77 |
| Just ahead | II | 126 |
| | | |
| Kings came riding | I | 81 |
| | | |
| Lie on this green and close your eyes — | II | 61 |
| Little trotty wagtail, he went in the rain | I | 75 |
| | | |
| Marjorie, sitting on the doorstep | II | 105 |
| Me and my horse go clippety cloppety | I | 23 |
| Mix a pancake | I | 4 |
| Mrs. Peck-Pigeon | I | 56 |
| Mud is very nice to feel | I | 55 |
| My aunt she died a month ago | II | 95 |
| My desk's at the back of the class | II | 99 |
| My hair's tightly plaited | II | 111 |
| My poor old bones — I've only two — | II | 86 |
| | | |
| Never go to France | I | 63 |
| New shoes, new shoes | I | 34 |
| Noah was an Admiral | I | 71 |

|  | Book | Page |
|---|---|---|
| Now, in the twilight, after rain | II | 59 |
| | | |
| O, my true love's a smuggler and sails upon the sea | II | 43 |
| 'O, where are you going to, my pretty little dear . . .? | I | 31 |
| O yea! O yea! O yea! | I | 4 |
| Oats and beans and barley grow! | I | 50 |
| Of all the Knights in Appledore | I | 105 |
| Oh, the times are hard and the wages low | II | 22 |
| Oh we can play on the big bass drum | I | 38 |
| Old King Cole | I | 40 |
| Old Mrs. Pettigrew | II | 107 |
| Oliver Cromwell's buried and dead | II | 21 |
| On a flat road runs the well-train'd runner | II | 101 |
| On these November evenings | II | 49 |
| On top of the Crumpetty Tree | II | 108 |
| Once Steeple Bumpstead | II | 25 |
| Once when the snow of the year was beginning to fall | II | 129 |
| One day when Father and I had been | I | 80 |
| Our train steams slowly in, and we creep to a stop at last | II | 48 |
| Out of his cottage to the sun | II | 47 |
| Out of the wood of thoughts that grows by night | II | 127 |
| Outside Bristol Rovers Football Ground | II | 129 |
| | | |
| Pistons, valves and wheels and gears | I | 6 |
| Poor Mrs. Utter | I | 92 |
| Rat-a-tat, Rat-a-tat! | I | 8 |
| Riddle cum diddle cum dido | II | 94 |
| Robert of Lincoln is gayly dressed | I | 19 |
| Round and round the roundabout | I | 3 |
| Rumbling in the chimneys | I | 5 |
| Run a little this way | I | 53 |
| | | |
| Sancta Maria, are they back yet again? | II | 118 |
| Scouring out the porridge pot | I | 5 |
| Sharp nose raised | I | 104 |
| Slowly the tide creeps up the sand | I | 44 |
| Soldier, soldier, won't you marry me . . . .? | I | 64 |
| Something told the wild geese | II | 128 |
| Spin a coin, spin a coin | I | 35 |
| Stocking and shirt | I | 98 |

| | Book | Page |
|---|---|---|
| Teacher, ring the children in | I | 32 |
| That ditch of rushes, is it deep | II | 83 |
| The black cat yawns | I | 76 |
| The boy climbed up into the tree | II | 78 |
| The City Financier | II | 56 |
| The crow goes flopping on from wood to wood | II | 61 |
| The day arrives of the autumn fair | II | 52 |
| The door swung inward. I stood and breathed | II | 76 |
| The droning roar is quickened, and we lift | II | 56 |
| The duck is whiter than whey is | I | 12 |
| The feathers of the willow | II | 47 |
| The flittermice are flitting | I | 17 |
| The fog comes | II | 100 |
| The horny-goloch is an awesome beast | II | 100 |
| The hunt is up, the hunt is up | II | 24 |
| The King of China's daughter | I | 90 |
| The King walked in his garden green | I | 65 |
| The long-rolling | II | 5 |
| The moon has a face like the clock in the hall | I | 78 |
| The night was coming very fast | II | 121 |
| The noise that annoys | I | 101 |
| The old King of Dorchester | II | 10 |
| The Owl and the Pussy-Cat went to sea | I | 14 |
| The piper came to our town | II | 20 |
| The scarlet buses splashed their way | II | 29 |
| The sea-gull curves his wings | I | 9 |
| The shepherds almost wonder where they dwell | II | 72 |
| The sun is a huntress young | II | 13 |
| The tide rises, the tide falls | II | 15 |
| The train goes running along the line | I | 28 |
| The wind breaks bound, tossing the oak and chestnut | II | 101 |
| The wind cracked his whip | I | 73 |
| The windows are open at Number One | I | 68 |
| There are big waves and little waves | I | 56 |
| There is an inn, a merry old inn | I | 113 |
| 'There is not much that I can do . . .' | II | 85 |
| There lived a wife at Usher's Well | II | 30 |
| There once was a man with a double chin | II | 12 |
| There was a man lived in the moon | I | 42 |
| There was a sage in days of yore | I | 61 |

|                                                              | Book | Page |
|--------------------------------------------------------------|------|------|
| There was a young lady of Sheen                              | II   | 93   |
| There was an old man in a barge                              | II   | 92   |
| There was an old man of Peru                                 | II   | 92   |
| There was an old man with a beard                            | II   | 92   |
| There was an old woman                                       | I    | 93   |
| There was no song nor shout of joy                           | II   | 84   |
| There was once a young man of Oporta                         | II   | 93   |
| There were a liddle piglet, he wadn't very old               | I    | 108  |
| There's a humming in the sky                                 | I    | 7    |
| There's many a pool that holds a cloud                       | II   | 125  |
| They rise like sudden fiery flowers                          | I    | 70   |
| They went to sea in a Sieve they did                         | II   | 6    |
| This is the superfluminous Osc                               | II   | 96   |
| This is the week when Christmas comes                        | I    | 18   |
| Through Dangly Woods the aimless Doze                        | II   | 98   |
| Today I think                                                | II   | 69   |
| 'Twas in the month of Liverpool                              | I    | 100  |
| Twinkle, twinkle little star                                 | II   | 112  |
|                                                              |      |      |
| Under the rose-tree's dancing shade                          | II   | 46   |
|                                                              |      |      |
| Waves lap lap                                                | I    | 9    |
| We be the King's men, hale and hearty                        | II   | 5    |
| We found a mouse in the chalk quarry today                   | II   | 77   |
| Welcome, red and roundy sun                                  | II   | 71   |
| What are you able to build with your blocks?                 | I    | 102  |
| What is this light here                                      | II   | 32   |
| What splendid names for boys there are!                      | I    | 87   |
| When bordering pinks and roses bloom                         | II   | 86   |
| When bread-and-cheese                                        | I    | 59   |
| When chestnuts are hanging                                   | II   | 112  |
| When coltsfoot withers and begins to wear                    | II   | 120  |
| When I was sick and lay a-bed                                | I    | 88   |
| When I went out                                              | II   | 116  |
| When the grass was closely mown                              | II   | 89   |
| When the sound of pigeons rises muted through glass          | II   | 51   |
| When Uncle John brought home the pig on Christmas afternoon  | I    | 115  |
| White is a dove                                              | II   | 68   |
| Why is it that the poets tell                                | II   | 64   |
| 'Will you take a walk with me . . .?'                        | I    | 15   |

|                                      | Book | Page |
| ------------------------------------ | ---- | ---- |
| With this round glass                | II   | 60   |
| Wynken, Blynken and Nod one night    | I    | 99   |
|                                      |      |      |
| You love the roses—so do I           | II   | 101  |

# Index of Authors

|  | Book | Page |
|---|---|---|
| ALDIS, DOROTHY |  |  |
| Clown, The | I | 14 |
|  |  |  |
| ALDRICH, THOMAS BAILEY |  |  |
| Tiger-Lilies | II | 16 |
|  |  |  |
| ANONYMOUS |  |  |
| Aiken Drum | I | 42 |
| Band, The | I | 38 |
| Cat came Fiddling, A | I | 4 |
| Cheerful Old Bear at the Zoo, A | II | 93 |
| Clucking Hen, The | I | 15 |
| Cowboy Spring | I | 23 |
| Dabbling in the Dew | I | 31 |
| Dance, Thumbkin, Dance | I | 48 |
| December | I | 4 |
| Gipsy Laddie, The | II | 17 |
| Here we come A-Piping | I | 2 |
| Here we go Round the Mulberry Bush | I | 49 |
| Horny-Goloch, The | II | 100 |
| Hunting Song | II | 24 |
| Lachlan Gorach's Rhyme | I | 54 |
| Leave her, Johnny | II | 22 |
| Month of Liverpool, The | I | 100 |
| My Aunt | II | 95 |
| My Bonny Lad | II | 84 |
| Oats and Beans and Barley | I | 50 |
| Old King Cole | I | 40 |
| Oliver Cromwell | II | 21 |
| Oranges and Lemons | I | 33 |

|  | Book | Page |
|---|---|---|
| ANONYMOUS—*continued* | | |
| Piper O' Dundee, The | II | 20 |
| Queen Nefertiti | I | 35 |
| Sampan | I | 9 |
| Smuggler, The | II | 43 |
| Soldier, Soldier | I | 64 |
| There was an Old Man of Peru | II | 92 |
| There was a Young Lady of Sheen | II | 93 |
| Twa Corbies, The | II | 85 |
| Whale, The | II | 23 |
| Wife of Usher's Well, The | II | 30 |
| Windy Old Weather | I | 22 |
| Wonders of Modern Science | II | 112 |
| | | |
| ASQUITH, HERBERT | | |
| Ship sails up to Bideford, A | II | 44 |
| | | |
| BAKER, BARBARA | | |
| Spike of Green, A | II | 116 |
| | | |
| BENNETT, RODNEY | | |
| Windy Nights | I | 5 |
| | | |
| BENNETT, ROWENA | | |
| Under the Tent of the Sky | I | 73 |
| | | |
| BENTLEY, E. C. | | |
| Dr. W. G. Grace | II | 95 |
| | | |
| BOYDEN, POLLY C. | | |
| Mud | I | 55 |
| | | |
| BRAHMS, CARYL | | |
| King's High Drummer, The | I | 27 |
| | | |
| BROOKS, PHILLIPS | | |
| Christmas Everywhere | II | 15 |
| | | |
| BRYANT, WILLIAM CULLEN | | |
| Robert of Lincoln | I | 19 |

|  | Book | Page |
|---|---|---|
| **CARROLL, LEWIS** | | |
| Obvious Reasons | II | 93 |
| | | |
| **CHALMERS, PATRICK R.** | | |
| Hay Harvest | II | 73 |
| | | |
| **CHURCH, RICHARD** | | |
| Cat, The | II | 106 |
| | | |
| **CLARE, JOHN** | | |
| Fairy Things | II | 70 |
| Flight of Birds, The | II | 61 |
| Little Trotty Wagtail | I | 75 |
| November | II | 72 |
| Wood-Cutter's Night Song, The | II | 71 |
| | | |
| **COATSWORTH, ELIZABETH** | | |
| Sea Gull, The | I | 9 |
| | | |
| **COLERIDGE, SARA** | | |
| Garden Year, The | I | 77 |
| | | |
| **CORNFORD, FRANCES** | | |
| Princess and the Gipsies, The | II | 27 |
| | | |
| **DAVIES, W. H.** | | |
| Fog, The | II | 124 |
| In Spring-Time | II | 125 |
| | | |
| **DE LA MARE, WALTER** | | |
| Berries | I | 93 |
| Fly, The | II | 87 |
| Magnifying Glass, The | II | 60 |
| Please to Remember | II | 104 |
| Quack! | I | 12 |
| | | |
| **DEHN, OLIVE** | | |
| November Morning | II | 51 |

|  | Book | Page |
|---|---|---|
| DICKINSON, EMILY | | |
| Snake, The | II | 119 |
| | | |
| DIXON, RICHARD WATSON | | |
| Song | II | 47 |
| | | |
| DODGE, MARY MAPES | | |
| Ho, Dandelion! | I | 26 |
| | | |
| DRINKWATER, JOHN | | |
| Moonlit Apples | II | 117 |
| | | |
| DYMENT, CLIFFORD | | |
| Banjo Player, The | II | 29 |
| | | |
| ELIOT, GEORGE | | |
| Roses | II | 101 |
| | | |
| FARJEON, ELEANOR | | |
| Boys' and Girls' Names | I | 87 |
| In the Week when Christmas Comes | I | 18 |
| Mrs. Peck-Pigeon | I | 56 |
| Outside | I | 104 |
| Scarecrow | I | 2 |
| Tailor | I | 13 |
| There are Big Waves | I | 56 |
| Wheelbarrow | I | 36 |
| | | |
| FIELD, EUGENE | | |
| Wynken, Blynken and Nod | I | 99 |
| | | |
| FIELD, RACHEL | | |
| Something Told the Wild Geese | II | 128 |
| | | |
| FISHER, AILEEN | | |
| After a Bath | I | 57 |
| | | |
| FLEMING, ELIZABETH | | |
| Steeple, The | II | 25 |

|  | Book | Page |
|---|---|---|
| **FRANKLIN, ALEXANDER** | | |
| Open Windows | I | 68 |
| Shepherds, The *(adapter)* | II | 32 |
| | | |
| **FROST, ROBERT** | | |
| Runaway, The | II | 129 |
| | | |
| **GARTHWAITE, JIMMY** | | |
| Engineers | I | 6 |
| | | |
| **GAY, JOHN** | | |
| Snail, The | II | 86 |
| | | |
| **GORELL, LORD RONALD** | | |
| London to Paris by Air | II | 56 |
| | | |
| **GOUGH, IRENE** | | |
| Song of the Year, The | I | 78 |
| | | |
| **GOULD, ELIZABETH** | | |
| Shining Things | I | 59 |
| | | |
| **GRAHAME, KENNETH** | | |
| Ducks' Ditty | I | 37 |
| | | |
| **GRAVES, ROBERT** | | |
| 'General Elliott, The' | II | 45 |
| | | |
| **GRAY, ALEXANDER** | | |
| On a Cat, Ageing | II | 87 |
| | | |
| **GREEN, MARY MCB.** | | |
| Aeroplane | I | 7 |
| | | |
| **HAMILTON, GEORGE ROSTREVOR** | | |
| Tugs | II | 60 |
| | | |
| **HARDY, THOMAS** | | |
| At the Railway Station, Upway | II | 85 |
| Marching Song | II | 5 |

|  | Book | Page |
|---|---|---|
| HARDY, THOMAS—*continued* | | |
| Oxen, The | II | 132 |
| Sheep Fair, A | II | 52 |
| | | |
| HARRISON, GREGORY | | |
| Priest's Hole | II | 118 |
| | | |
| HERBERT, A. P. | | |
| At the Theatre | II | 80 |
| | | |
| HERRICK, ROBERT | | |
| Down with the Holly, Ivy, All . . . | II | 74 |
| | | |
| HOLMES, NOEL | | |
| Here we Come Gathering! | I | 32 |
| | | |
| HOOD, THOMAS | | |
| French and English | I | 63 |
| | | |
| HOWITT, MARY | | |
| Fairies of the Caldon Low, The | I | 109 |
| | | |
| JARRELL, RANDALL | | |
| Bats | II | 102 |
| Owl | II | 120 |
| | | |
| KINGDON-WARD, WINIFRED | | |
| Bats | I | 17 |
| | | |
| KIRKUP, JAMES | | |
| Lonely Scarecrow, The | II | 86 |
| | | |
| LEAR, EDWARD | | |
| Jumblies, The | II | 6 |
| Owl and the Pussy Cat, The | I | 14 |
| Quangle Wangle's Hat, The | II | 108 |
| There was an Old Man in a Barge | II | 92 |
| There was an Old Man with a Beard | II | 92 |
| | | |
| LINDON, J. A. | | |
| Sink Song | I | 5 |

|  | Book | Page |
|---|---|---|
| LINDSAY, VACHEL | | |
| Indian Summer on the Prairie, An | II | 13 |
| Mysterious Cat, The | I | 46 |
| LONGFELLOW, HENRY WADSWORTH | | |
| Tide Rises, The Tide Falls, The | II | 15 |
| LOWELL, AMY | | |
| Wind and Silver | II | 100 |
| MacCAIG, NORMAN | | |
| Granton | II | 42 |
| McCORD, DAVID | | |
| Every Time I Climb a Tree | I | 96 |
| MILLER, MARY B. | | |
| Cat | I | 76 |
| MILNE, A. A. | | |
| Knight Whose Armour Didn't Squeak, The | I | 105 |
| MOORE, ROSALIE | | |
| Catalogue | II | 54 |
| MORLEY, CHRISTOPHER | | |
| Smells | II | 64 |
| MORTON, J. B. | | |
| Dancing Cabman, The | II | 14 |
| NEWBOLT, HENRY | | |
| Toy Band, The | II | 9 |
| NORRIS, LESLIE | | |
| Ballad of Billy Rose, The | II | 129 |
| NOYES, ALFRED | | |
| Daddy Fell into the Pond | I | 95 |
| Shining Streets of London, The | II | 59 |

|  | Book | Page |
|---|---|---|
| 'OLD SHEPHERD' | | |
| Bold Piglet, The | I | 108 |
| | | |
| O'NEILL, MARY | | |
| What is Grey? | II | 67 |
| What is White? | II | 68 |
| | | |
| O'SULLIVAN, SEUMAS | | |
| Piper, A | II | 2 |
| | | |
| POPE, J. | | |
| Noise | I | 86 |
| | | |
| REED, ALASTAIR | | |
| Names for Twins | I | 65 |
| | | |
| REEVES, JAMES | | |
| Ceremonial Band, The | II | 10 |
| Doze, The | II | 98 |
| Fireworks | I | 70 |
| Hippocrump, The | I | 82 |
| Mr. Tom Narrow | I | 103 |
| Mrs. Utter | I | 92 |
| Noah | I | 71 |
| Osc, The | II | 96 |
| Run a Little | I | 53 |
| Slowly | I | 44 |
| Stocking and Shirt | I | 98 |
| Three Singing Birds, The | I | 65 |
| Under Ground | II | 88 |
| Village Sounds | II | 61 |
| | | |
| RICHARDS, LAURA | | |
| Kindness to Animals | II | 94 |
| | | |
| ROETHKE, THEODORE | | |
| Bat, The | II | 117 |
| | | |
| ROBERTS, ELIZABETH MADOX | | |
| Christmas Morning | I | 116 |
| Hens, The | II | 121 |

**ROBERTS, MICHAEL**
Gale Warning                                    II              101

**ROBERTS, PETER**
Target Area                                     II              126

**ROSSETTI, CHRISTINA**
Pancake, The                                    I               4

**SANDBURG, CARL**
Fog                                             II              100

**SANSOM, CLIVE**
Apple Song                                      I               30
Conjuror                                        I               21
Conkers                                         II              112
Dachshund                                       I               104
Dustman, The                                    I               8
Engine Driver, The                              I               28
Martha of Bethany                               II              123
Policeman, The                                  I               101
Postman, The                                    I               8
Roundabout, The                                 I               3

**SCRIVEN, R. C.**
Marrog, The                                     II              99

**SERRAILLIER, IAN**
Anne and the Field-Mouse                        II              77
Helicopter, The                                 II              116

**SITWELL, EDITH**
King of China's Daughter, The                   I               90

**SQUIRE, J. C.**
Ship, The                                       II              84

**STEPHENS, JAMES**
Apple Tree, The                                 II              81
Fifteen Acres, The                              II              2
Main-Deep, The                                  II              5
White Fields                                    I               69

|                                       | Book | Page |
|---------------------------------------|------|------|
| STEVENS, DAVID                         |      |      |
| Old Zip Coon                           | II   | 12   |
|                                       |      |      |
| STEVENSON, ROBERT LOUIS                |      |      |
| Autumn Fires                           | I    | 70   |
| Block City                             | I    | 102  |
| Dumb Soldier, The                      | II   | 89   |
| Land of Counterpane, The               | I    | 88   |
| Moon, The                              | I    | 78   |
| Visit from the Sea, A                  | II   | 115  |
| Where go the Boats?                    | I    | 91   |
|                                       |      |      |
| STRONG, L. A. G.                       |      |      |
| Old Dan'l                              | II   | 47   |
|                                       |      |      |
| STRUTHER, JAN                          |      |      |
| Policeman, The                         | II   | 110  |
|                                       |      |      |
| STUART, DOROTHY MARGARET               |      |      |
| Fugitive, The                          | II   | 83   |
|                                       |      |      |
| SUMMERS, HAL                           |      |      |
| Rescue, The                            | II   | 78   |
|                                       |      |      |
| SWENSON, MAY                           |      |      |
| Water Picture                          | II   | 58   |
|                                       |      |      |
| TENNANT, PAMELA                        |      |      |
| Moon Magic                             | I    | 80   |
|                                       |      |      |
| THACKERAY, W. M.                       |      |      |
| Sage's Pigtail, The                    | I    | 61   |
|                                       |      |      |
| THOMAS, EDWARD                         |      |      |
| Cock-Crow                              | II   | 127  |
| Digging                                | II   | 69   |
|                                       |      |      |
| THORLEY, WILFRID                       |      |      |
| Song for a Ball-Game                   | I    | 58   |
|                                       |      |      |
| TODD, BARBARA EUPHAN                    |      |      |
| Sing a Song of Honey                   | I    | 24   |

|  | Book | Page |
|---|---|---|
| TOLKIEN, J. R. R. | | |
| Man in the Moon stayed up Too Late, The | I | 113 |
| | | |
| TYNAN, KATHARINE | | |
| August Weather | II | 55 |
| | | |
| WALSH, JOHN | | |
| Arrival, The | II | 48 |
| I've got an Apple Ready | II | 111 |
| Marjorie Sitting on the Doorstep | II | 105 |
| New Boy, The | II | 76 |
| On these November Evenings | II | 49 |
| Out at Night | II | 107 |
| Peter to Tea | II | 74 |
| Skipping Song | I | 59 |
| Sweet Chestnuts | II | 114 |
| | | |
| WATSON, WILLIAM | | |
| Ballad of Semmerwater, The | II | 19 |
| | | |
| WHITMAN, WALT | | |
| Runner, The | II | 101 |
| | | |
| WILDE, OSCAR | | |
| Painting, The | II | 42 |
| | | |
| WILLIAMS, CHARLES | | |
| Kings came Riding | I | 81 |
| | | |
| WOLFE, fFRIDA | | |
| Choosing Shoes | I | 34 |
| Uncle John's Pig | I | 115 |
| | | |
| WOLFE, HUMBERT | | |
| Thrushes | II | 56 |
| | | |
| YOUNG, ANDREW | | |
| Cuckoos | II | 120 |